FLORENCE

Travel Lovers' Library

Each in two volumes profusely illustrated

Florence
  By GRANT ALLEN

Romance and Teutonic Switzerland
  By W. D. McCRACKAN

Old World Memories
  By EDWARD LOWE TEMPLE

Paris
  By GRANT ALLEN

Feudal and Modern Japan
  By ARTHUR MAY KNAPP

The Unchanging East
  By ROBERT BARR

Venice
  By GRANT ALLEN

Gardens of the Caribbees
  By IDA M. H. STARR

Belgium: Its Cities
  By GRANT ALLEN

Rome
  By WILLIAM TAYLOR FIELD

Romantic Ireland
  By M. F. MANSFIELD

L. C. PAGE & COMPANY
Publishers
200 Summer Street, Boston, Mass.

BENVENUTO CELLINI-PERSEUS.

FLORENCE

By
Grant Allen

IN TWO VOLUMES

Vol. II.

ILLUSTRATED

Boston
L. C. Page & Company
MDCCCCII

Copyright, 1901
BY L. C. PAGE & COMPANY
(INCORPORATED)

All rights reserved

Colonial Press
Electrotyped and Printed by C. H. Simonds & Co.
Boston, Mass., U. S. A.

CONTENTS.

CHAPTER		PAGE
I.	THE PIAZZA DELLA SIGNORIA	1
II.	THE LONG CORRIDOR OF THE UFFIZI	12
III.	THE RENAISSANCE PAINTINGS OF THE UFFIZI	31
IV.	THE FIRST HALL OF THE TUSCAN SCHOOL AND THE TRIBUNE	52
V.	THE HALLS OF THE FOREIGN SCHOOLS AND THE FIRST HALL OF THE VENETIAN SCHOOL	64
VI.	THE SECOND HALL OF THE VENETIAN SCHOOL AND THE EARLY FLORENTINE PAINTINGS	80
VII.	THE SCULPTURE IN THE UFFIZI	93
VIII.	THE PITTI PALACE	107
IX.	THE PITTI PALACE CONTINUED	129
X.	THE BARGELLO	145
XI.	OR SAN MICHELE	177
XII.	SAN MINIATO	190
XIII.	THE ETRUSCAN MUSEUM	204
XIV.	THE RESIDUUM	215

LIST OF ILLUSTRATIONS.

VOLUME II.

	PAGE
BENVENUTO CELLINI. — PERSEUS (*see page 6*) *Frontispiece*	
COURT OF THE PALAZZO VECCHIO	5
LOGGIA DEI LANZI	8
SIMONE MARTINI AND LIPPO MEMMI. — ANNUNCIATION	18
DON LORENZO MONACO. — ADORATION OF THE MAGI	23
BICCI DI LORENZO. — ST. COSIMO AND ST. DAMIAN	24
PIERO DI COSIMO. — ANDROMEDA	29
GHIRLANDAJO. — ADORATION OF THE MAGI	32
LORENZO DI CREDI. — ANNUNCIATION	36
BOTTICELLI. — STRENGTH	40
SODOMA. — ST. SEBASTIAN	48
BOTTICELLI. — CALUMNY	53
RAPHAEL. — MADONNA DEL CARDELLINO	57
HOLBEIN. — PORTRAIT OF RICHARD SOUTHWELL	65
TITIAN. — FLORA	71
MANTEGNA. — ADORATION OF THE MAGI (Central panel of the Triptych)	73
BOTTICELLI. — ADORATION OF THE MAGI	88
BOTTICELLI. — BIRTH OF VENUS (Detail)	90

List of Illustrations.

	PAGE
TRIBUNA (Uffizi Gallery)	100
HALL OF NIOBE (Uffizi Gallery)	104
PITTI PALACE	108
SEBASTIANO DEL PIOMBO. — MARTYRDOM OF ST. AGATHA	115
RAPHAEL. — MADONNA DEL GRANDUCA	116
FRA BARTOLOMMEO. — DEPOSITION	122
TITIAN. — MAGDALEN (Detail)	129
ALBERT DÜRER. — EVE	132
ANDREA DEL SARTO. — YOUNG ST. JOHN THE BAPTIST	134
BARGELLO (Palazzo del Podestà)	146
DONATELLO. — ST. GEORGE	154
GIOVANNI DA BOLOGNA. — MERCURY	166
LUCA DELLA ROBBIA. — MADONNA	169
VERROCCHIO. — VIRGIN AND CHILD	174
GIOVANNI DA BOLOGNA. — ST. LUKE THE EVANGELIST	179
GHIBERTI AND MICHELOZZO. — ST. MATTHEW	181
SAN MINIATO DEL MONTE	190
FAÇADE OF THE BASILICA OF SAN MINIATO DEL MONTE	194
DONATELLO. — BUST OF ST. LAWRENCE	217
MICHAEL ANGELO. — DAWN (Detail of Monument of Lorenzo de' Medici)	220
MASACCIO. — HEAD OF CHRIST (Detail of Tribute Money)	222
FILIPPINO LIPPI. — MADONNA APPEARING TO ST. BERNARD	233
ANDREA DELLA ROBBIA. — A BABY	237

Florence.

CHAPTER I.

THE PIAZZA DELLA SIGNORIA.

THE centre of modern Florence is occupied by the Piazza della Signoria, which contains the Palazzo Vecchio and the Loggia dei Lanzi. This square was once the Forum of the Republic, and around it revolved the political and social life of early Florence.

In the thirteenth century the Bargello (to be visited later) was the seat of the Florentine Government. But in 1298, about the same time when Santa Croce and the Cathedral were rising above their foundations, the City began to feel the want of a second stronghold for its new democratic (or oligarchic) authorities, and of a fitting hall for its deliberative assemblies.

In that year, therefore, the Signoria commissioned the great Arnolfo di Cambio, who was already engaged in building the Duomo, to begin the erection of a vast castle, now known as the Palazzo Vecchio. It was evidently based in idea upon the Palazzo Pubblico in the rival town of Siena, the foundations of which appear to have been laid some nine years earlier. The greater part of the building as it now stands represents Arnolfo's original work, though the upper portion of the slender tower is of the fifteenth century, while the façade toward the Via del Leone at the back was added by Vasari in 1540. The courtyard and porch have also suffered great alterations.

The Palazzo Vecchio in its original form was strictly the Castle of the Guilds of Florence, which had imposed their rule in the thirteenth century over the whole city. It was, in short, the stronghold of the commercial oligarchy. The early government of Florence had been mainly aristocratic, and all its functions were performed by the nobles; but by 1282, the Arts or Guilds, among which the Wool-Weavers and Silk-Workers were the most important members, had gained possession of the executive power, which they entrusted to their own Priori or Guild-Masters. The body thus installed in the Palazzo Vecchio was known as the Signoria: it retained power in Florence until the gradual rise of the democratic despotism of the Medici, a wealthy commercial family who favoured the people, and finally made themselves, in the sixteenth century, Grand Dukes of Tuscany. (See Villari.) The fortress-like appearance of the Palace is due to the fact that the commercial oligarchy had to hold its own by force within the city against the great nobles on the one hand, and popular rising on the other. All Florence, in fact, is clearly built with a constant eye to internal warfare.

In 1376 the Piazza della Signoria was further decorated by the erection of the Loggia dei Lanzi, a magnificent vaulted arcade for the performance of public functions before the eyes of the citizens. This noble building was perhaps designed by Orcagna, but was certainly carried out by Benci di Cione and Simone di Francesco Talenti. It exhibits the same curious combination of round arches with Gothic detail which is also seen in the neighbouring church of Or San Michele — the chapel of the Guilds.

The arcade was known at first as the Loggia de' Priori or della Signoria; it gained its present name under Cosimo I., who stationed here his German lance-men.

I do not advise a visit to the interior of the Palazzo Vecchio until after you have seen everything else of importance in Florence, when Baedeker's account will be amply sufficient. But a cursory inspection of the exterior, and of the general features of the Piazza, is necessary to an understanding of Florentine history. As you will already have seen in the picture at San Marco, Savonarola was burnt at the stake in this square, near the spot now occupied by the Fountain of Neptune.

Go along any street, as far as the Duomo: then, turn down the Via Calzaioli. On your right, as you turn the corner, is the beautiful little Loggia of the * Bigallo, probably designed by Orcagna, and built in 1352. Notice here the peculiar Florentine combination of round arches with Gothic architecture. The statues over the front, toward the Piazza, by Filippo di Cristoforo, represent a Madonna and Child, flanked by St. Dominic and St. Mary Magdalen.

COURT OF THE PALAZZO VECCHIO.

The Piazza Della Signoria. 5

Continue down the Via Calzaioli till you come to the Piazza della Signoria. Observe the façade of the Palazzo Vecchio. Then enter the outer court, built by Michelozzo (whose hand you will now recognise) in the Renaissance style, in 1432. The elaborate decorations were added in 1565; though very florid, they have a certain picturesqueness which is not unpleasing. The centre is occupied by a charming little * fountain, by Verrocchio, representing a Boy on a Dolphin. The surrounding sculptures, as well as those at the door, are by inferior Renaissance artists, and quite uninteresting. So is Bartolommeo Ammanati's great fountain, in the square, with Neptune and Tritons. The equestrian * statue (in bronze) of Cosimo I., by Giovanni da Bologna, is scarcely more interesting. It has high technical merit, but lacks grace or beauty.

(Michael Angelo's David stood till recently at the door of the Palazzo Vecchio. So did the Marzocco, at present in the Bargello.)

Now, turn to the Loggia dei Lanzi. Note the noble sweep of the large round arches, and the character of the decorations. Observe its resemblance (on a larger scale) to the Bigallo.

The figures on the frieze above are after designs by Agnolo Gaddi, and are fine examples of the characteristic Gothic allegorical personages, with incipient Renaissance leanings. They represent Faith, Hope, Charity, Temperance, and Fortitude. Identify the symbols with an opera-glass.

Of the pieces of sculpture within the Loggia, by far the most important are the two bronzes.

The one facing the Piazza, to the left of the steps, is ** Benvenuto Cellini's Perseus, — one of the most perfect works of its kind ever cast in metal. The lightness and delicacy of the workmanship, the airy coquettish grace of the young hero, as he holds aloft the head of the slaughtered Medusa, have never been equalled in their own peculiar bravura manner. The work, however, is rather that of a glorified artistic silversmith than of a sculptor properly so called. You can see in every line and limb that the effects aimed at, — and supremely attained, — are those of decorative metal-work, not those of greater bronzes and marbles. Cellini has here transcended the proper limits of his peculiar art; and he has done so triumphantly. The result justifies him. Stand and look, long and often, at this perfect marvel of technical excellence. When you have exhausted the central figure, turn to the reliefs and statuettes at the base, also by Cellini. (The relief in front, * Perseus rescuing Andromeda, is a copy; the original you will see when you visit the Bargello.) The * four admirable figures in the niches represent respectively, Jupiter (Zeus), the father of Perseus; Danaë, his mother; Minerva (Athene); and Mercury (Hermes), both of whom befriended him. (Read up the story in a classical dictionary, if you do not already know it.) The Latin verses on the base are neat and appropriate.

The second bronze, round the corner toward the Uffizi, is * Donatello's Judith, with the head of Holofernes, erected in front of the Palazzo Vecchio after the expulsion of the Medici. It bears the inscription, "Salutis Publicæ Exemplum." The work, however, is heavy and confused, and shows that Donatello had not yet wholly mastered the art of modelling for bronze-casting. The reliefs below are better, especially that of * Cupid and Psyche.

The other sculpture in the Loggia is of less importance. By the steps are two lions; to the right, an antique; to the left, one by Flaminio Vacca. Under the arch, on the right, is a marble group of the *Rape of the Sabines, by Giovanni da Bologna, with good *relief beneath it. Within, left, is a modern group of the Rape of Polyxena, by Fedi, not wholly unworthy of the company in which it finds itself. In the centre, is the *Dying Ajax (or perhaps, Menelaus with the body of Patroclus) a good antique, probably a Greek original; another example of the same exists at Rome, where it is known as Pasquino. This replica has been greatly restored. On the right is a frigid Hercules slaying the Centaur Nessus, by Giovanni da Bologna. By the back wall are five antique portrait-statues of Vestals or Priestesses: together with a *heroic barbarian female figure, known as the Thusnelda (the third on the left), and remarkable for its powerful expression of grief on a fine half-savage countenance.

In visiting the Uffizi, you proceed round the corner from the Loggia dei Lanzi, and enter a spacious quadrangle, a narrow oblong in shape, and open at the side toward the Palazzo Vecchio. The Palazzo degli Uffizi, which girdles this quadrangle, was erected as public offices

LOGGIA DEI LANZI.

HOLBEIN. — PORTRAIT OF RICHARD SOUTHWELL.

The Piazza Della Signoria.

(whence the name) by Vasari, in 1560, and completed by Alfonso Parigi, in 1580. Round the lower floor runs a continuous arcade, the Portico degli Uffizi, the niches of which, after remaining long empty, have been adorned in our own time with a series of marble statues of distinguished Tuscans, all named below, which it is well worth while some day to go round and inspect or identify. The building contains, in its lower portion, the Post Office, the Central Archives of Tuscany, and the National Library; but of course to the visitor its chief importance is derived from the picture gallery and sculpture on the upper floor.

The collections in the Uffizi are, on the whole, the most important and valuable in Florence. In painting, it is true, the gallery contains fewer fine works of the great Early Renaissance artists than does the Belle Arti; but on the other hand, it is rich in paintings by Raphael, it has some noble designs by Leonardo and Fra Bartolommeo, and it represents more fully than the rival gallery the pictorial art of the High Renaissance. Moreover, it is not confined to Tuscan and Umbrian works (to which nevertheless I advise you in Florence mainly to address yourself) but has some admirable North Italian and Venetian specimens, by Mantegna, Titian, Giorgione, and others. Outside Italy altogether, it also embraces some noble Flemish, German, and Dutch works, which it will be impossible for you to pass by wholly unnoticed. Then, finally, it has in addition its collection of sculpture, including several famous works, once unduly over-praised, as well as many antiques, less celebrated in their way, but often more deserving of serious attention. I have endeavoured to note in passing the most important of all these various treasures, giving most attention, it is true, to Tuscan and Umbrian handicraft, but not neglecting the products of other schools, nor the antique sculpture.

As everywhere, my aim here has been purely explanatory. If at times I have diverged into an occasional expression of æsthetic approbation or the opposite, I hope the reader will bear in mind that I never pretend to do so with authority, and that my likes and dislikes are merely those of the average man, not of the professed critic.

Do not attempt to see all the Uffizi at one visit, or even any large part of it. Begin with

The Piazza Della Signoria.

a little bit, and examine that thoroughly. Do not try to combine the paintings and sculpture in any one room; observe them separately on different occasions. Follow for each class the general order here given; you will then find the subject unfold itself naturally. Study Baedeker's excellent plan of the rooms before you go in. Recollect that the galleries extend, in three arms, right round the top floor of the entire building, as seen from outside; this will help you to understand the ground-plan of the rooms, as well as the charming glimpses and views from the windows.

A passage, built quaintly over houses and shops, and distinguishable outside, crosses the Ponte Vecchio from the Uffizi to the Pitti. It was designed by the Medici as a means of intercommunication, and also as a place of possible escape in case of risings or other danger. You can cross by means of it from one gallery to the other; but you must pay an extra franc for entrance in the middle.

CHAPTER II.

THE LONG CORRIDOR OF THE UFFIZI.

APPROACH from the Piazza della Signoria. The entrance is by the second door under the portico on the left hand side of the Uffizi Palace. (The statues and busts on the staircase and in the vestibule, etc., will be treated separately, with the other sculptures.)

The Long Gallery, which we first enter, contains for the most part early works in painting, many of which are of comparatively slight artistic importance. I advise you to begin with the paintings alone, not attempting to combine them with the sculpture in the same day. Turn to the right on entering the gallery, and start at the end of the room with the oldest pictures.

Number 1 is a Græco-Byzantine Madonna, of the tenth century, interesting as representative of the starting-point of Italian art. It should be compared with 2, an Italian picture aiming

The Long Corridor of the Uffizi.

at the same style (twelfth century), which again leads up (at a distance) to the Cimabue in Santa Maria Novella. Observe the superior technique of the Byzantine. These early Madonnas deserve close attention.

Number 3 is a Crucifix, where the position of the Madonna and St. John on the ends of the arms is highly characteristic: the type survives till quite a late period. By its sides are small scenes from the Passion, the types in which should be carefully noted. The face of the St. Peter, for example, in the upper left compartment, already strikes a key-note; while the Christ in Limbo, delivering Adam and Eve from the jaws of death, contains all the salient elements which you will find, improved and transformed in later versions. Note in crucifixes the point where the two separate nails in the feet, seen in this example and the next, are replaced by the single nail, a later representation. Observe also whether the eyes are open or closed.

Number 4 has the same devices of towers and canopies, to mark towns and interiors, to which I have already called attention in the barbaric Magdalen at the Belle Arti.

Number 6, a Crucifix with the single nail, has

the position of St. John and the Virgin well marked on the cross-pieces. The pelican feeding her young above is symbolical. It recurs often. I do not dwell upon these very early works, as they lack artistic interest; but the visitor who takes the trouble to examine them in detail, as well as the Madonnas in their neighbourhood, will be repaid for his trouble. For example, 5, by Guido da Siena, an important early Sienese master, marks decided advance upon 2, and leads the way to the later Sienese manner, which is already present in embryo in this picture.

In 7, do not overlook Peter and Paul, and St. Catherine between the wheels, in the predella.

The next, 8, is a fine altar-piece, attributed to Giotto, of the Agony in the Garden, where the angel with the literal cup and the three sleeping Apostles are highly characteristic of the type. You have seen them elsewhere in later examples. Note the little figure of the donor at the side. The Kiss of Judas and the Parting of the Raiment in the predella must not be omitted.

Number 9 is a Florentine altar-piece, where the Madonna and Child are flanked by the patron of the city, St. John the Baptist, and the local bishop, San Zanobi, identifiable by the Florentine lily on his morse or buckle.

Then, 10, St. Bartholomew enthroned, with his usual knife, and angels recalling the manner of Cimabue, was of course painted for an altar dedicated to the saint. Note these saints enthroned, in the same way as Our Lady, often with other saints forming a court around them.

Beside it are two Giottesque Crucifixions, in the first of which, 13, the position of the Madonna, the Magdalen, and St. John, and the angel catching the sacred blood, will by this time be familiar. In the second, 12 (a Crucifix), note the gradual approximation to reality in the altered positions of Our Lady and St. John as contrasted with those in earlier Crucifixions.

Number 11 is again a Florentine Madonna, with the two local saints, John the Baptist and Zanobi, a mandorla of cherubs, and angels holding the Florentine lily. Note that this is sometimes represented by the white lily and sometimes by the iris.

Number 14 is an altar-piece of the school of Orcagna, St. John the Evangelist, enthroned, with his eagle by his side, trampling on the vices, in a fashion which is characteristic of Dominican painting. They bear their names: Pride, Avarice, Vainglory. Notice, above, the characteristic Christ, holding the Alpha and Omega. You will do well to spend a whole morning (if you can spare the time), in attentive study of these first fourteen numbers. They cast floods of light on subsequent painting.

Beyond the door is 17, an Ascension of St. John the Evangelist; an altar-piece closely suggested by Giotto's fresco in Santa Croce. Compare with photographs.

Above it, 15, by Pietro Lorenzetti, is a characteristic and gentle Sienese Madonna. Compare it with Guido's Number 5. Observe the placid Sienese angels, with their somewhat ill-humoured mouths, drawn fretfully downward, a survival from the morose Byzantine severity. Very early art is never joyous. The inscription is curious, because in it, as in most pictures of the school of Siena, the panel itself speaks in the first person — So-and-so painted me.

Number 16, the story of the Anchorites in the Desert, by Pietro Lorenzetti, is partly reminiscent of the great fresco in the Campo Santo

The Long Corridor of the Uffizi. 17

at Pisa. Most of its many episodes you will find explained in Mrs. Jameson. It takes much studying.

Above, 26, is a good altar-piece by Bernardo Daddi; St. Matthew, St. Nicholas of Bari. Nicholas was the name of the donor.

From this point the technical excellence of the pictures increases rapidly. 20, St. Cecilia, patroness of music, once wrongly attributed to Cimabue, is a good and stately Giottesque figure, for her altar in her old church at Florence, now destroyed. Round it are eight (habitual) stories of her life. On the left side, in the first is her wedding feast (note the music); in the second she reasons with her husband, Valerian, in favour of virginity; in the third an angel crowns Cecilia and Valerian; in the fourth Cecilia converts her husband's brother, Tiburtius. On the right side, in the fifth picture, is the baptism of Tiburtius; in the sixth, Cecilia's preaching; in the seventh, her trial before a Roman Court; and in the eighth, her martyrdom in flames in her bath. All are quaintly and interestingly treated. See Mrs. Jameson.

The altar-piece above has its name inscribed on it. Its types are worth study.

Number 23, ** Simone Martini and Lippo Memmi, the Annunciation, is one of the loveliest altar-pieces of the early school of Siena. The exquisite angel, to the left, bears a branch of olive (beautifully treated) instead of the more usual lily, which, however, stands in a vase to separate him from the Madonna. Note the words of the Salutation (raised in gold) issuing from his mouth, and the inscriptions on his charming flowing ribbons. Do not omit the exquisite work of his robe. Our Lady herself, seated in a dainty inlaid chair, representative of the finest ecclesiastical furniture of this period, shrinks away, as often. The book and curtain are habitual. The Madonna's almond-shaped eyes and somewhat fretful drawn-down mouth still faintly recall Byzantine precedents. But the mild Sienese spirit and fine painting of the piece are admirable. Do not overlook the dove escorted in the centre in a mandorla of cherubs, and the three arches isolating the personages. Linger long over this masterpiece. To the right and left are two patron saints of Siena, Sant' Ansano and Saint Juliet, with their palms of martyrdom. Here, again, in the inscription, the picture speaks. Compare this exquisite

SIMONE MARTINI AND LIPPO MEMMI. — ANNUNCIATION.

altar-piece in all its details with previous works of the school of Siena. It is one of the loveliest things in this gallery.

In 22, observe the Annunciation, above, in two compartments; the coat of arms; and the singular inscription, "Hear the other side," probably betokening it as a votive offering from a party to a quarrel, in opposition to some other already dedicated. (The official catalogue refers it to some court of justice.)

Number 27, attributed to the (doubtful) painter Giottino, is a very fine Deposition from the Cross, reminiscent in its principal figures of the Giotto at Padua. The saints to the right, showing the nails, may be well compared as to attitude with the great Fra Angelico at the Belle Arti. To the left are two donors, with their patrons placing their hands on their heads. The one in white is St. Benedict: the other I take to be, not San Zanobi, but St. Remi (Remigio), from whose church the picture comes.

Number 28 is an Agnolo Gaddi, Annunciation, where the loggia, book, dove, vase with lilies, and other particulars, should all be noted. This is an unusually good specimen of its artist. The little scenes in the predella will by this time explain themselves. Note that an interior is still represented by taking out one side of the building. Compare the Adoration and the Presentation with others seen previously. (A Presentation, by the way, can always be distinguished from a Circumcision by the presence of Simeon and Anna, the former of whom usually holds the divine infant.

Number 29, Niccolò di Piero Gerini's Coronation of the Madonna, with attendant group of Florentine patron saints, comes from the Mint of Florence. You will recognise the Baptist; Santa Reparata (with her red cross flag); San Zanobi; St. Anne, holding the town of Florence; St. Catherine with her spiked wheel; St. Joseph with the budded staff; St. John the Evangelist on the right holding his Gospel; St. Matthew on the left holding his, with the first word inscribed, etc.

Number 30, the Doubting Thomas of the school of Agnolo Gaddi, is a characteristic treatment.

Number 31 is another Coronation of the Virgin. The saints are named. Note their characteristics. The one you may fail to recognise is St. Ivo, who is in Florence the patron of orphans. Observe the combination of Francis and Dominic. In the *cuspidi* is an Annunciation, in two portions.

Number 36 is another Annunciation, of the school of Orcagna. Here the division, such as it is, is made by means of the arches. Unless I mistake, two separate panels have here been united. This often happens in Annunciations.

Number 32 is an altar-piece by Giovanni da Milano, with group of named saints. Below are choruses of Virgins, Martyrs, Patriarchs, etc. All have their names. Note their characteristics. The picture was painted for the church of Ognissanti (All Saints), whence the assemblage. Catherine and Lucy often go together. The latter has two symbols, both significant of her name: a flame, or her eyes in a dish. Originally only emblems to suggest the name, these marks have later legends attached to them. The two holy martyrs, St. Stephen and St. Lawrence, buried in the same grave, also go together. See in Mrs. Jameson the quaint story of how Lawrence, "the courteous Spaniard," turned over on his side to give the best place to the earlier martyr. In the last of the group, the scallop-shell of St. James marks him as the saint to whose great shrine (Santiago de Compostella) pilgrims make religious journeys. The dove at St. Gregory's ear we have often before noted. I cannot too strongly recommend study of such named saints and choruses for identification afterward. Notice among those below: Reparata, with her flag; Agnes with her lamb; and Margaret with her dragon, among the Virgins; Noah with his ark, among the Patriarchs, and so forth. The Prophets hold distinctive verses in the Vulgate from their own writings. Above, in small circles, the Lord creating heaven and earth.

Number 35, St. Martin dividing his cloak with the beggar, is a common French subject, rarer in Italy.

Number 40 is a Pietà, by Lorenzo Monaco, with symbolical figures, in the background, of Pilate washing his hands; the sacred coat; Judas receiving the money; the knife that cut Malchus's ear; Peter and the servant; the sun and moon darkened; the pelican and its young; the crowing cock; the lance of St. Longinus; and many other symbols, the rest of which I leave to the reader. Puzzle it out in detail.

DON LORENZO MONACO. — ADORATION OF THE MAGI.

Do not pass by 37, Spinello Aretino, and others, merely because I do not mention them. (In this picture for example, the halo round the head of St. Longinus, the devil carrying away the soul of the impenitent thief, the parting of the raiment, etc., should all be noticed. The last scene usually occupies the right-hand side in historical as opposed to devotional pictures of the Crucifixion. Observe in future which scene is intended.)

Number 39 is by *Don Lorenzo Monaco, an Adoration of the Magi; a fine picture, with the usual long sinuous bodies and drapery of that peculiar painter. Observe, to the right, the attendants seeing the star and struck with wonder. Also, the Moors in the suite, and the very imaginative camels. I have treated of this picture at much greater length in an article in the *Pall-Mall Magazine* on Adorations in general. The scenes above are by a later hand; observe the very graceful Annunciation.

Number 41, also by Don Lorenzo Monaco, is a fine Tabernacle, in its original frame, with Madonna and Child, named saints, and Annunciation. Observe, in almost all these early Madonnas, the draped infant, and note the point where the nude commences.

Number 43, Zanobi Strozzi's Giovanni de' Medici, is interesting chiefly as an early portrait of the shrewd old founder of that great family.

Number 44, by the same painter, represents St. Lawrence enthroned on his gridiron; below, episodes of his legend. To the right, he releases souls from Purgatory — a hint to pray to him for friends in torment.

Number 45, by *Bicci di Lorenzo, is of Cosimo and Damian, the two Medici saints, with their medical instruments and boxes of drugs. The attitudes, I think, are partly suggested by a Byzantine original, though the technique and treatment are of course Florentine of the period. Below, in the predella, are two quaint little stories — the miracle of the Moor's leg, and the decapitation of the holy doctors.

Number 46 is a Madonna Enthroned, with St. Philip and St. John the Baptist.

Number 48 is a Madonna and Child, with, on the left, St. John the Baptist of Florence and St. Francis with the Stigmata; on the right, the Magdalen and St. John the Evangelist; and in the *cuspidi*, St. Peter and St. Paul.

BICCI DI LORENZO. — ST. COSIMO AND ST. DAMIAN.

Close by, 49 and 50, are interesting little panels of St. Catherine standing on her wheel, and St. Francis on a symbolical desert.

Number 51 is a Florentine Madonna, with St. John the Baptist, Anthony Abbot, Peter, Lawrence. Note, on the frame, the usual symbols of the Magdalen and St. Catherine.

Here is the door to the First Tuscan Room, which pass for the present, and continue on along the Long Corridor.

Number 52, by Paolo Uccello, a cavalry battle, is interesting as showing his early attempts at movement of horses, foreshortening, etc. This is very bad. His picture in the National Gallery shows an immense advance on this early effort. Observe particularly the hard task he has had in trying to foreshorten the dead horses in the foreground.

Number 53, by Neri di Bicci, is a characteristic Annunciation, on the same model as those in the Belle Arti. Garden, bedchamber, and all details, are conventional. This is better painted, however, than is usual with Neri.

Near by is a Madonna of the school of Verrocchio, with characteristic Florentine type of the period.

Number 56, by Pesellino (or more probably Baldovinetti), is an Annunciation, with the angel just entering. This somewhat unusual point should be noted. Also, the attitude of the Madonna, reminiscent of Donatello's treatment. The porphyry arcade is also interesting. The cypresses recur. Never pass by an Annunciation unnoticed.

Number 54 is a wooden Madonna, by Neri di Bicci, with angels of the same material drawing the curtain, and child opening a pomegranate.

Number 60, Madonna and Child, with Florentine and Medici saints, by Baldovinetti, is interesting as a specimen of its rare painter, who aimed at certain effects unusual in his period. Cosimo and Damian may be compared with the previous picture in this gallery by Bicci di Lorenzo. Then, notice St. John the Baptist, now growing youthful: he is generally young for the High Renaissance. Beyond, is St. Lawrence, with his gridiron embroidered on his deacon's robe as a symbol: he represents Lorenzo de' Medici; behind him St. Julian for Giuliano de' Medici. Next, are St. Peter Martyr and St. Anthony Abbot, joint patrons of Piero de' Medici; to balance St. Peter Martyr, St. Francis, kneeling. A very family picture, with Franciscan and Dominican suggestions. The cypresses in the background, common elements in such scenes, may be compared with many other adjacent pictures of the period or earlier. This was once a good hard picture, but it has been badly treated. Compare with 56 for technical method.

Number 62, I note mainly as being a rare secular picture of its period.

In 63, Cosimo Rosselli's Coronation of the Virgin, the utter want of sacredness in its angels' faces is conspicuous. The technique, though hard, has this painter's merits. Note the triple crowns on the two chief personages.

Number 65, by the same painter, is an Adoration of the Magi, where the Florentine portraits to the left are noteworthy. This is, indeed, a picture painted for the sake of its portraiture. The curious character-study in the St. Joseph is worth notice. Observe the tendency toward greater truth in the landscape background.

Number 79 is perhaps by Botticelli; a dainty Tuscan Madonna, with typical face, in clouds with angels.

Numbers 69, 70, 71, 72, 73, are five somewhat insipid figures of Virtues by Pollaiolo, much injured. The Renaissance frieze and decorations are noteworthy.

Number 64 is amply described on its frame; a good hard picture.

Number 84, by Piero di Cosimo, is one of that painter's favourite mythological scenes, — the Marriage of Perseus. Observe the composition and treatment. We here get a new note struck by the Renaissance, both in painting and architecture.

Above it, 75, is a charming unknown Tuscan Madonna. Observe in the Madonnas, etc., of this group the increasing nudity of the infant.

Number 80, of the school of Ghirlandajo, is a good hard Madonna and saints. You will recognise St. Blaise with his wool-carder, St. Anthony of Padua, St. Benedict, and St. Antony Abbot. Bishop Blaise is the patron of the wool-trade, one of the staple businesses of mediæval Florence.

Beyond this, unnumbered, are two fine pictures by Luca Signorelli, noticeable for their study of the nude and their anatomical knowledge. Luca is in this respect, as in many others,

PIERO DI COSIMO. — ANDROMEDA.

the precursor of Michael Angelo. Art for art's sake is his theory. The shepherds in the background are there only because Luca likes to paint them.

Numbers 81 and 83 show Piero di Cosimo in two very different moods. The Andromeda is most characteristic. Piero delighted in these grotesque and incongruous monsters. In the Madonna picture, the eagle marks St. John the Evangelist; the lily, St. Anthony of Padua; the keys, St. Peter; the cross, San Filippo Benizzi (?); then St. Catherine and St. Margaret, kneeling in the foreground.

Number 90 is an example of the beginning of the Decadence, a Peruginesque Madonna, in a mandorla, adored by the saints who foreshadow the seventeenth century. The St. Francis in front leads on to the insipid church pictures of the Baroque period. The others are the Baptist, Jerome, and Anthony Abbot.

Notice also 91, by Gerino da Pistoia, a Madonna and Saints. I call attention to this picture mainly in order that you may judge for yourself whether the exquisite Cenacolo di Fuligno in the Via Faenza (to be visited later) can really be attributed to this insipid and jejune artist. The San Rocco to the **right showing** the wound in his leg is a characteristic figure of the painter. The other saints **are** easily recognised.

In this Long Corridor you have just been able to trace the gradual development of Tuscan art (for the most part as seen in its second or third rate representatives) from the earliest date down to the High Renaissance. We will now proceed into the rooms which contain the worthier representatives of the great age of the early Renaissance. Do not, however, neglect the early works; without them, you can never intelligently understand the later ones.

CHAPTER III.

THE RENAISSANCE PAINTINGS OF THE UFFIZI.

RETURN along the Corridor to the first open door marked Scuola Toscana. Pass through the first room, and enter the second, opposite, the Sala Terza, which contains the pictures that come first in chronological order among the later painters. This room you cannot study too long. It embraces the finest work of the best period.

On the wall to the left, as you enter, is Jacopo (Landini) da Casentino's brilliantly coloured Glory of St. Peter, seen enthroned as Pope, with stories from his life on either side. The attendant saints and church dignitaries to whom he distributes honours are symbolical: examine them. Note St. Cosimo. The group of Peter in prison, visited by the angel, to the left, is interesting both in itself and for comparison with the noble Renaissance work in the Brancacci chapel at the Carmine. (Go from one to the other.) To the right is the crucifixion of Peter; at the ends, eight Apostles or Evangelists, Andrew, John, Philip, Matthew, Thomas, the Jameses, Luke.

Above it, 1315, by Mainardi, are beautiful figures of three saints, of whom the chief, St. Stephen, enthroned, is an exquisite modification of the traditional type; beside him, James and Peter.

Number ** 1285 is a beautiful Annunciation, recently attributed to Leonardo: if so, an early work. Note here again how the traditional features are all retained, including even the garden and the cypresses in the background (so frequent in early works), while the whole spirit of the scene is transformed and transfused with the developed artistic ideas of the Renaissance. Observe the exquisite sculpture of the prie-dieu. Our Lady's hands are not Leonardesque. They recall rather the school of Botticelli. This debatable picture may be by Ridolfo Ghirlandajo: but whoever painted it, it is very beautiful.

Number 1295, * Ghirlandajo's round Adoration of the Magi, is one of this great painter's masterpieces; admirably balanced and richly

GHIRLANDAJO. — ADORATION OF THE MAGI.

coloured. The Madonna and Child, the Three Kings in the foreground, and the Joseph should all be closely noted. Observe the attitudes and actions of the Kings. Their faces are clearly portraits. So are the shepherds, with clear-cut features (as of Florentine scholars and humanists), in the group to the right, and the delicate lads with Medici faces, near the sheep and horses in the background. Notice the beautiful ruined temple, with its conventional shed or stable, and the ox and ass close by, as well as the admirable painting and foreshortening of the horses. The composition, though full, is admirable; the colour most harmonious. Every detail of this picture, one of the finest specimens of Renaissance art, should be carefully studied, both for comparison with others, and as a specimen of its artist's consummate skill.

I have dealt with this also at greater length in the *Pall-Mall Magazine*, on the subject of Adorations.

Number 1301, by Antonio Pollaiolo, is St. James, with his pilgrim's hat and staff, flanked by St. Vincent and St. Eustace. The central saint in such groups is of course the important one. These are fine characteristic figures by this good but not very sympathetic painter. He thinks more of anatomy and portraiture than of soul or sacredness. The colour is splendid. The St. Vincent here may well be compared with his brother deacon St. Stephen, in the Mainardi opposite. The picture was painted for the Chapel of St. James (of the Cardinal of Portugal) at San Miniato.

Number 1311, by * Lorenzo di Credi, "Touch Me Not," represents Christ and the Magdalen in the garden. A beautiful specimen of the tender and finished painting of this exquisite artist, who always succeeds best in small subjects. Observe the delicate and clear-cut landscape in the background, which should be compared with the mistier and more poetical effect of the mountains in Leonardo's Annunciation beside it. Contrast also the painting of the robe of Christ with the Madonna's bosom and the angel's sleeve in the (doubtful) Leonardo, which last are as well done as it is possible to do them. Lorenzo's painting has always the distinctness of a bas-relief.

In number 1300, by Piero della Francesca, are good hard portraits (named) in the dry and formal profile manner of this excellent Umbrian

The Renaissance Paintings. 35

painter; at the back (swung by a hinge), an allegorical triumph of the same personages: the duchess drawn by unicorns, the symbol of chastity. Where sufficient information is given on the frames I do not repeat it.

Number 1313, Lorenzo di Credi, Christ and the Woman of Samaria, is good, but not quite so satisfactory as its companion picture. Beneath this is a fine predella by Luca Signorelli, admirable as indicating the aims of the artist.

On the entrance wall, beside the door, ** 1160, by Lorenzo di Credi, an Annunciation, is a most beautiful Renaissance revivification of somewhat the same early type as that often reproduced by Neri di Bicci (see the Long Gallery). Observe the admirable way in which the traditional motives are here retained and beautified. There is nothing new, but everything is altered with subtle charm. The attitude and expression of the angel, and the little start of the Madonna, all copied from the Giottesque, are most admirable in their wholly different treatment. Note at the same time how much more closely Lorenzo has followed the traditional ideas than Leonardo (if it be Leonardo) has done. Even the little round windows you will frequently find in earlier treatments; but the clear drawing, the dainty colour, the fairy-like scene, the exquisite delicacy of the technique, are all Lorenzo's own. So is the beautiful landscape seen through the windows. There are four Annunciations in this room, two of them by Lorenzo. Compare them carefully, in order to mark coincidences and differences. Also, compare the other Lorenzos here. Nowhere else in the world will you see him all at once to equal advantage. You cannot linger too long over this delicious picture.

Number 1307, a ** Filippo Lippi, is a Madonna and Child, the infant supported by two merry boy-angels. Note the folds of the transparent stuff in Our Lady's head-dress. This is an exquisite picture, representing the same general types as the Coronation of the Virgin in the Belle Arti. It is perhaps Filippo's most charming panel work. There is little to understand in it, but worlds to look at. Return to it again and again till it has burnt itself into your memory. It was painted for Cosimo Pater Patriæ, and stood originally as an altar-piece in a room in the Medici (Riccardi) Palace. The Madonna is the most perfect embodiment of

LORENZO DI CREDI. — ANNUNCIATION.

Lippi's ideal. The angels are delicious. Even the chair-arm is a poem. As for the colour, it is exquisite.

Above it, 1287, is a round Madonna and Child, by Lorenzo di Credi. This is a type of subject commonly known as the Madonna adoring the Child: you will meet it often. Observe the infant St. John of Florence, sustained by an angel. (See how the Renaissance alters St. John.) The ruined temple and Joseph sleeping in the background (to suggest night) are all conventional. As usual, Lorenzo is less successful on this larger scale than in his smaller pictures: he loses by expansion. Only the Child here is quite worthy of his genius. Compare carefully with the infinitely more beautiful Annunciation beneath it. Yet, if any one else had painted it, it would have been a masterpiece. We judge Lorenzo by Lorenzo's standard.

Number 1223, by Franciabigio, is a Temple of Hercules, interesting chiefly as a specimen of these curious Renaissance resuscitations of classical subjects. It was the front of a chest, to contain a bride's trousseau.

Above it, 1303, is a ** Botticelli, exquisitely beautiful Madonna and Child, enthroned, in a niche. In this picture again there is nothing to explain, but much to admire and wonder at. The type of Our Lady is one of Botticelli's most spiritual conceptions.

Number 1314, by ** Lorenzo di Credi, is another beautiful little Annunciation, with the motives considerably varied on the preceding one, but scarcely less beautiful. You will observe by this time that Annunciations fall into different types, and that works in each type are suggested by predecessors. In this delicious and clear little picture, observe the attitude and hand of the kneeling angel; the adoring wonder and joy of the Madonna; and the beautiful landscape in the background, dainty and pure as always with Lorenzo. But observe, also, the constant survival of the loggia, the dividing pillar, and the bed in the background. This is a simple treatment, but exquisitely effective.

Number 1168, by Lorenzo di Credi, Madonna and St. John, with charming landscape background, is a beautiful work, not quite, however, attaining the level of the two Annunciations. This Mater Dolorosa is of course represented after the Crucifixion. Lorenzo succeeds best with isolated figures, as in this room, and the

Louvre altar-piece; where he attempts composition, he loses in beauty.

Above these, 1291, is a *Luca Signorelli, a Holy Family, in which the springs of Michael Angelo's art can be distinctly seen. As technique, this picture is of great interest. Observe the masterly treatment of the drapery. It is interesting to contrast the type of colouring in this work, in the Lorenzo, and in the supposed Leonardo, — which last, whoever painted it, is a glorious piece of colouring.

Below, in a predella, notice the quaint little Sienese stories from the life of Benedict, redolent of the naïveté of place and period. In the centre, as a child, he mends his nurse's broken platter; on the left he dwells in penitence at the grotto of Subiaco; on the right he is visited at Monte-Cassino by King Totila.

The right wall is devoted to four exquisite pictures by Botticelli. In the centre is an *Annunciation, in some ways resembling in motive two others in the room, the kneeling Gabriel recalling the second Lorenzo di Credi, while the attitude of the Madonna highly resembles the first; but the difference in technique and conception is immeasurable. There is not a detail in this liquid-flowing drapery that is not instinct with Botticellian feeling. The attitudes of the hands should be compared with the Three Graces in the Primavera. The landscape background may be contrasted with Lorenzo. The coincidences and differences in these pictures will help you toward a conception of the painter's manner. Movement is the key-note of Botticelli's art.

On either side of it are two round pictures, also by Botticelli. That to the left, ** 1267 bis, is an inexpressibly lovely Coronation of the Virgin, where the attendant angels represent Medici children. About this picture I have nothing to say. It can only be left to the silent admiration and gratitude of the spectator.

To the right, 1289, is * a Madonna enthroned, with the Child (lumpy) bearing a pomegranate. The adoring angels also suggest Medici portraits. The atmosphere and feeling of the whole picture are exquisite.

To the extreme right and left on the wall are two companion allegorical figures, * Strength, by Botticelli, and Prudence, by Pollaiolo. These pictures, being painted as companion pieces, afford an excellent opportunity for contrasting

BOTTICELLI. — STRENGTH.

The Renaissance Paintings.

the spirit of the two painters. They belong to the same series as those in the Long Corridor.

On an easel in this room is ** Fra Angelico's Coronation of the Virgin, an often copied picture, with exquisite groups of adoring saints. After our study of this painter at the Belle Arti, however, its characteristics will sufficiently reveal themselves by inspection. It deserves long notice as one of the most beautiful of the master's easel pictures. It comes from the Church of Santa Maria Nuova. A couple of dozen saints may be recognised.

Now, enter the room through which you have already passed, Scuola Toscana, Seconda Sala. This room contains for the most part works of the High Renaissance, tending toward the decadence. Some are of the first order of merit, but many are quite inferior in interest to those in the hall we have just quitted.

Beginning at the left as you enter, is 1271, by Bronzino, Christ Releasing the Souls from Hades. In this tasteless and empty work, only the formal elements belong to the early conception; the whole spirit and sacredness of the scene has disappeared; the composition is vapid. The Christ, still bearing his traditional white flag with the red cross, is treated merely as an excuse for painting the nude, as are most of the other figures round him: and very ugly nude Bronzino makes of them. The Saviour seizes by the hand a brown bald-headed Adam, whom one recognises only by the aid of earlier pictures. The semi-nude women and boys of the foreground are painted entirely for their naked limbs, with the empty art of Bronzino, and with his usual pallid, unnatural flesh-colours. The colouring of all the draperies is also as bad and as crude as it can be. It is curious, in this typical High Renaissance picture, with its false and affected art, to catch glimpses here and there of the earlier saints and patriarchs, with reminiscences of their conventional symbols. The work is mainly interesting as a study in the springs of the decadence. Compare it with the great and noble Christ in Limbo of the Spanish Chapel.

Next to it, 1269, is a Vasari, portrait of Lorenzo the Magnificent, a good picture of its sort, but chiefly interesting as a portrait illustrating the mean and petty character of the man it represents.

Number 1270, by Pontormo, is a good portrait of Cosimo I., in the brilliant reds which this painter loved, and which doubtless here represent in part the traditional costume of St. Cosimo, patron saint of the grand duke and his family. Compare with the work opposite, 1267, also by Pontormo, a companion portrait (not contemporary) of Cosimo Pater Patriæ, the founder of the family greatness, in the dress which you will now recognise as being that of St. Cosimo, the holy doctor, as seen in the Bicci di Lorenzo of the Long Corridor. The portrait was, of course, modernised by Pontormo from earlier contemporary pictures.

Between these two is **Andrea del Sarto's beautiful Madonna and Child, raised on a pedestal, supported by two charming baby angels, and flanked on either side by St. Francis and St. John the Evangelist. They are almost devoid of symbols. Compare the exquisitely soft and blended colour of this noble and touching work with the crudity and vulgarity of the contrasted pigments in Bronzino's Hades. These saints represent perhaps the highest development of the ancient type of altar-piece in which Our Lady is attended by two saints, one on either hand, in formal attitudes. The evolution of the composition in this set of subjects is a most interesting study. Our Lady's face, the Child, the draperies, the St. John, and his red cloak, are all as lovely as art can make them. In the St. Francis, just a note obtrudes itself of the coming degeneracy. He is a faint trifle affected. But, oh, what colour!

Beyond it, 1266, good portrait by Bronzino, showing him in one of his happier moments.

Number 1265 is a design in bistre by Fra Bartolommeo for a Madonna and Child, with St. Anne behind. The position of the St. Anne is conventional; see the Leonardo in the Louvre; in other pictures in Florence the Madonna sits on her mother's lap. On either side stand the patron saints of Florence, conspicuous among whom are Santa Reparata and San Zanobi. This work, much praised by the critics for its skilful composition, seems to me to strike the first note of the decadence. The adoring face of St. Anne, however, is undeniably beautiful. Observe the survival of her traditional head-dress. The saint was a popular favourite in Florence, as Walter de Brienne was expelled from the city on St. Anne's Day, which was ever afterward kept as a public holiday. The picture was commissioned by the town of Florence.

The Renaissance Paintings. 45

On the back wall, 1261, by Jacopo da Empoli, shows St. Ivo as protector of orphans; a good late picture, painted for the magistracy of the orphans, of which the saint was patron. You will find a rude early picture of the same subject in the Opera del Duomo, interesting for comparison: St. Ivo wears a similar dress in both. Above it is one of Pontormo's ugliest nudes.

Number 1268, by ** Filippino Lippi, is an exquisite but somewhat sad-faced Madonna, crowned by angels. The clear and luminous colour strikes the eye at once. In the foreground is a fine ascetic figure of St. John the Baptist of Florence, balanced by San Zanobi, distinguishable by the Florentine lily on his morse. In the background, St. Augustine (the authorities say, St. Victor) and St. Bernard. Observe the beautiful Renaissance architecture and the charming faces of the angels. The flowers also are lovely. Above are the arms of the Florentine people. This great work was painted for a hall in the Palace of the Signoria; hence the grouping, and the Florentine arms at the summit.

Number 1257, ** Filippino Lippi's exquisite Adoration of the Magi, is a work instinct with

Renaissance feeling. The Old King has already presented his gift, which is held by an attendant on the right. The Middle-aged King, close shaven, kneels behind him. The Young King, as often, is just taking his gift in his hand, while his crown is being removed by a servant, as in earlier pictures. But the movement and characterisation of the scene are entirely Filippino's. All the figures are portraits, some of them are Medici. The group of the Madonna and Child, with the yellow-robed St. Joseph bearing his staff, has been entirely transformed from earlier models by the painter's genius. The attendants to the right are particularly noteworthy. Even the conventional accessories of the ruined temple, the shed, the ox and ass, and the cavalcade in the distance, are all transfused with Filippino's own sympathetic temperament. This is one of the culminating pictures of the best age of the Renaissance: stand long before it. Observe the hands and feet, and the management of the drapery.

On the right wall, 1283, is an Entombment, a good hard work by the little-known late Renaissance painter Raffaello di Franco (Botticini), conspicuous for its extraordinary want of

The Renaissance Paintings. 47

emotion. The figures look as if an entombment were an every-day occurrence with them. The Florentine St. John the Baptist marks the country of the painter. In the background is the Way to Calvary.

Number 1281 bis, is a Cosimo Rosselli, Madonna and Child with the infant St. John; even harder and drier than is the painter's wont. To the right and left of her are St. James as pilgrim, and St. Peter with his keys. The hands and feet are the best part of the picture. Compare the solid angels holding the crown with the charmingly living and flowing figures in the Filippino to the left of it. The drapery is good.

Over the door is a * Granacci, the Madonna letting fall the Sacra Cintola to St. Thomas. The charmingly youthful figure of the saint was evidently suggested by Nanni di Banco's admirable relief on the north door of the Cathedral, itself suggested by the Orcagna at Or San Michele. To the right St. Michael the Archangel kneels to balance St. Thomas. In the empty sarcophagus are flowers as usual — this time roses, not lilies. This is Granacci's masterpiece, and is an astonishingly fine example for such a painter.

Number 1252 is * Leonardo's unfinished Adoration of the Magi, in bistre. Compare with the Filippino. A fine work, full of Leonardesque power, but without sufficient detail to render it attractive to the general observer.

Number 1279 is * Sodoma's celebrated St. Sebastian, shot with arrows. This is one of the most beautiful representations of the subject, in a very low tone of colour, and is perhaps Sodoma's masterpiece. The angel descending in a glory behind with a crown of martyrdom is peculiarly full of Sodoma's spirit. Fully to appreciate it, however, you must know the master's other works at Siena. This panel, painted for a Sienese Society, was carried in procession as a plague picture by the Confraternity to which it belonged. On the back is a Holy Family, with St. Sigismund, and the other great plague saint, San Rocco. An attendant will unlock it for you.

Number 1278 bis is an example of the school of Verrocchio, good Madonna, with St. John of Florence, San Zanobi holding a model of the town and cathedral, St. Francis with the Stigmata, and St. Nicolas of Bari with his three balls. The architecture and decoration are note-

SODOMA. — ST. SEBASTIAN.

worthy. Observe also the palms and cypresses in the background, which often appear in similar pictures.

Numbers 1277 and 1275 represent two miracles of San Zanobi, and are by Ridolfo Ghirlandajo, son of Domenico; from the church of the Fraternity of San Zanobi. These two pictures, like Granacci's Sacra Cintola, indicate the extraordinary way in which, during the great age of Florentine art, even secondary painters often produced works of the highest merit. Nothing can be better in its way than their drawing, composition, and colouring. The first represents the miracle of the tree which burst into leaf when the body of San Zanobi was being carried past it (see the Cathedral). Observe its naked boughs, and the leaves just draping them. Note the Baptistery on the right (without the later sculpture) and the tower of the Palazzo Vecchio; to the left, the Campanile and part of the old façade of the Cathedral. The second picture shows the miracle of the restoration of the French (or Gallic) lady's son, which is also the subject of Ghiberti's relief on the Arca of San Zanobi in the Cathedral. Observe the Florentine lily on San Zanobi's morse and the good portraits of bystanders. The colour here is beautiful; the grouping fine; and the air of returning life on the child's pallid face very well rendered.

Number 1259, * Mariotto Albertinelli's Visitation, is another splendid example of the way in which comparatively minor artists produced noble works, in the full flush of the High Renaissance. In composition this picture resembles somewhat the Ghirlandajo of the same subject in the Louvre, and far more closely the central part of the Pacchiarotto in the Belle Arti. Compare these two, and note the way the figures are silhouetted against the sky in the background. The design is said to be by Fra Bartolommeo. I have traced the evolution of the arch in the background in one of my papers in the *Pall-Mall Magazine*. Observe the survival of the traditional hoods in both St. Elizabeth and Our Lady. This picture, however, shows the way in which the beautiful brocades and other carefully wrought stuffs of early painting, well discriminated and reproduced, give place with the High Renaissance to what is known in the abstract as "drapery" — mere colour and folds, without distinctive texture. Observe this trait in this room, progressively, in the Filippinos, the Andrea del Sartos, the Albertinelli, and the Pontormo.

Next the door, * 1254, is an Andrea del Sarto, St. James, with his pilgrim's staff, as protector of children; a processional work, carried as a banner by the Confraternity of St. James, which protected orphans, and thus much injured. It now displays comparatively little of Andrea's delicate colouring.

On easels in the centre are two recent acquisitions: * 3452, Lorenzo di Credi's Venus, a fine treatment of the nude, not in colour quite equal to this artist's general level; and 3436, an Adoration of the Magi, drawn by Botticelli, but coloured, and spoiled in the colouring, in the seventeenth century. Little of the master remains, except the sense of movement and the character in some of the faces. The distinctive Botticellian feeling has almost gone out of it.

CHAPTER IV.

THE FIRST HALL OF THE TUSCAN SCHOOL AND THE TRIBUNE.

THE little room to the right, the Scuola Toscana, Prima Sala, contains an immense number of small works of various ages, many of which are of the first importance.

On the entrance wall, near the window, 1163 and 34, are *two admirable portraits by Lorenzo di Credi. Notice in the first the hands of a born sculptor, and the sense of form about the eyes and forehead. The second is that of a high-born and unscrupulous Florentine gentleman, a dangerous rival in a love-affair.

Number * 1178, Fra Angelico's Adoration of the Virgin, is a beautiful little work, highly typical in its arrangement. In the background is the Temple; in front, the High Priest, clad in his robe and ephod. To the right is the youthful figure of Our Lady, timid and girlish, accompanied by St. Anne and the Virgins of the

BOTTICELLI. — CALUMNY.

Lord, with the usual group of children in the distance; to the left St. Joseph with his budded staff, on which sits the dove of the Holy Spirit; behind him, as always, the angry suitors striking, and the impatient suitors breaking their staffs; and to the extreme left, the golden and silver trumpets. Even the garden wall at the back, with its palms and cypresses, is a conventional feature. You will find it in several earlier pictures. Compare the Taddeo Gaddi in Santa Croce, where almost every figure occurs in the self-same order. I have treated this subject at length in one of my articles in the *Pall-Mall Magazine*.

Number 1182, * Botticelli's Calumny, one of this great painter's finest though less pleasing works, is painted after the description of a picture by Apelles. The fine nude figure to the left recalls the Primavera. So does the beautiful form scattering roses over the nude man in the centre. The admirable Renaissance enrichment of the architecture, and the reliefs of the tribune must not be overlooked. This is a work which requires long study. The drapery of the woman in the foreground, to the extreme right, is a marvel of colouring.

Above it are three good little pictures, the finest of which, 1162, by Fra Angelico, is one of a series of the Life of John the Baptist, and represents Zacharias writing, "His name is John."

Number 1152 is a good small Fra Bartolommeo.

Number 1184, a * Fra Angelico, represents the death of the Madonna, attended, as usual, by the apostles and angels, with Christ in a mandorla receiving her glorified spirit. The apostles have their names inscribed on their haloes. Identify them. The little angels at the side are in Fra Angelico's most charming manner.

Number 1245, by Jacopo da Empoli, is a good Sacrifice of Abraham, somewhat reminiscent of Sodoma. Most of the other pictures on this wall require some attention.

Number 1156, ** Botticelli's Judith, with the head of Holofernes, is a marvellous work, deserving long study. No other painter ever put so much life and motion into his figures.

Beyond the door are some of Bronzino's unpleasing nudes.

A detestable Cigoli of St. Francis receiving

the Stigmata, and other unpleasing works of the same period, are also here.

On the end wall is an interesting Martyrdom of St. Sebastian. The type is the same as that of the Pollaiolo in the National Gallery, and the rude old work in the Opera del Duomo.

Beneath it, 1146, attributed to Andrea del Sarto, is a Madonna and Child with the infant St. John; not a pleasing specimen.

Number 1312 is another of Piero di Cosimo's fantastic monsters.

Number 1150, of the school of Pinturicchio, is a Madonna, with St. Joseph and St. Blaise; the latter easily recognised by his wool-carder.

Return along the right wall, passing by more nudes by Bronzino, and a little Visitation of the seventeenth century, interesting to compare with the Albertinelli, tolerable nudes by Zuccheri, and 1209, an unspeakably vulgarised Dead Christ by Bronzino; then, a Leda with the Swan, and other works, the best of their type, but singularly unpleasing.

Beyond the door, 1179, is a pretty little St. Sebastian by Botticelli. Number 1180 is a small copy of Allori's fine Judith in the Pitti. Number 1159 is a head of Medusa, unaccountably attributed to Leonardo. Number 1161 is an exquisite little Circumcision and Nativity by Fra Bartolommeo. On the back of the flaps is an Annunciation, in two separate pieces. Number 1157 is *a fine portrait, attributed to Leonardo. Number 1158 is by *Botticelli, Holofernes discovered headless under his tent. Above these are three fine portraits, of which that by *Masaccio is very remarkable. The medallist (1154), falsely called Pico della Mirandola, is probably a Botticelli. Higher still are good later portraits, by Andrea del Sarto, etc.

I have passed lightly over the small works in this room because they are so numerous; but many of them deserve the closest attention. Do not think because a picture is little it is unimportant. Some of the loveliest gems of the collection are in this small apartment.

The next room, the Tribuna, contains what are generally considered the gems of the collection, though the selection by the authorities is in accordance with the taste of the beginning of this century rather than with that of the present generation. Start at the door, entering from the main corridor. Left of the entrance is a Holy Family by Alfani; a trivial work, chiefly

RAPHAEL. — MADONNA DEL CARDELLINO.

interesting as showing the mixed school of Perugino and Raphael.

Number 1129, ** Raphael's Madonna del Cardellino, is one of the most beautiful pictures of his Florentine period (1507). It should be compared with the Belle Jardinière in the Louvre. The subject is one originally peculiar to Florentine painters, the Madonna and Child with the infant St. John of Florence, the latter here holding the symbolical goldfinch. Note how the earlier abstractness here gives way to a touch of naturalism. The exquisite sweetness and Florentine cast of the Madonna's countenance, and the charming painting of the nude boys should be carefully noted. This, however, is one of those pictures which must be mainly left to the perceptive powers of the reader. Do not overlook the charming contrast of the baby foot with the mother's in the foreground.

Number 1127 is by Raphael, or more probably from a design by Raphael; the Young St. John in the Desert. Here the Renaissance love for the healthy youthful nude male form has triumphed over the asceticism of earlier conceptions. This is just a beautiful boy, with the traditional attributes of the penitent in the desert. The Florentine St. John is often thus used as a mere excuse for earthly painting or sculpture. You will meet him again in many shapes at the Bargello.

Above it are 1130 and 1126, by Fra Bartolommeo, Job and Isaiah, grand, or shall I say rather, grandiose figures which reveal the spiritual parentage of the Raphael cartoons. These are typical specimens of this great but unpleasing High Renaissance painter, art, not spirit, and the art itself chilly.

Number 1125, by Franciabigio, the Madonna of the Well, has the same subject as the Raphael which balances it, but with the later Roman treatment, the spirituality all going out, and mere naturalistic prettinesses substituted for the careful painting and more spiritual ideals of the earlier epoch. A good work of its sort, but oh, how fallen!

Number 1124 is a *very fine portrait by Francia.

Beneath it, 1123, probably by Sebastiano del Piombo, is the so-called Fornarina, attributed to Raphael. By whomever produced, this is a splendidly drawn and well-painted but ugly and vulgar picture. Compare it with number 1120, by * Raphael, a beautiful portrait of an unknown lady, in his earlier and better manner. The attribution is doubtful: it has been ascribed to Leonardo.

Number 1121, by * Mantegna, is a fine portrait of the Duchess of Urbino. Above the door is a good Rubens.

Number 1115 is a * fine Van Dyck. Number 1117, * Titian's Venus, is a beautiful voluptuous nude, of a type suggested by the Giorgione now at Dresden. Compare with photographs.

Number 1136, by Veronese, is a very Venetian Holy Family, with a voluptuous fair-haired Venetian lady as St. Catherine. You can only know her for a saint because she carries a palm of martyrdom. Characteristic of the later lordly school of Venice.

Number 1131 is one of the replicas of Raphael's Julius II. (some say the original). There is a better one in the Pitti, and a third in the National Gallery.

Number 1141 is ** Dürer's Adoration of the Magi. Here in Florence I will not dwell in detail on this noble German work, which may however be compared in all its details, for likenesses and differences, with Italian representations. The face of the Madonna and of the Middle-aged King are essentially and typically German. The whole work, indeed, is redolent of German as opposed to Italian feeling: yet Dürer largely influenced contemporary Italians. In northern art, by the way, and as a rule in Lombardy and Venice, the Young King is a Moor. Note how in this picture almost all the traditional elements remain the same, yet how totally they are varied by the divergent spirit of the northern artist. Study of this picture and the Filippino in a neighbouring room is a fine lesson in the differences between German and Italian methods.

Number 1122, by * Perugino, is a beautiful Madonna and Child, with the St. John the Baptist of Florence, and the wounded St. Sebastian, — therefore, a plague picture. There is a fine replica of the last pathetic figure in the Louvre. This and Sodoma's are the most beautiful St. Sebastians ever painted. Perugino's is pure Umbrian in clearness and pietism: Sodoma's has the somewhat affected softness and glowing light of that Sienese Lombard.

Number 197 is a * fine portrait by Rubens of his wife; extremely natural.

Number 1114 is Guercino's Sibyl, astonished to find herself in such strange company.

Number 1108, a second Recumbent Venus by Titian, more simply voluptuous and more resembling Palma Vecchio's type than the former one, is good, but fleshly: it foreshadows Veronese. Beneath it are pictures of the later period, masterpieces, no doubt, in their own florid way, but sadly out of keeping with the Perugino, the Dürer, and the Raphael of the Cardellino.

Number 1143 is the Crown of Thorns, by Lucas van Leyden.

Number 1116, a *portrait of Beccadelli by Titian, is admirable but not pleasing. The flesh and hands are splendidly painted.

Number 1139 is **Michael Angelo's Holy Family with about as much holiness in them as there was in the painter; a magnificent work, on an uncongenial subject. Our Lady is a fine vigorous woman of the lower orders, with an unpleasing face, and splendid arms and hands, excellently painted. The pose of her neck is wonderful. The Child is not a divine figure, but a fine study in anatomy and foreshortening. The baby St. John of Florence in the background is a charming young Bacchus. The graceful nude figures behind, disposed in glorious attitudes, show what Michael Angelo really cared for. This is a triumphant work of art, but it none the less exhibits the futility of setting such a man to paint what were thought to be sacred pictures. Note the draperies.

Above are a fine Van Dyck and two Cranachs (Adam and Eve), interesting as showing the crude northern conception of the unidealised nude, very well rendered. Compare this Eve, in its faithful likeness to a commonplace undraped model, with Lorenzo di Credi's graceful Venus in an adjacent hall, or with the two voluptuous Titians in this very room. Compare the Adam, again, with Perugino's St. Sebastian. They mark the difference between the literal simplicity of the north and the idealism and daintiness of the south.

Number 1118, Correggio's Repose on the Flight into Egypt, with St. Francis adoring, is not a pleasing specimen of the great master. Far more interesting and typical is his 1134, * the Madonna adoring the Child, a pretty Parman woman, charmed with her baby. It has all that mastery of light and shade, and that

Tuscan School and the Tribune. 63

graceful delicacy of workmanship, which is peculiar to Correggio. But the simper is affected, and the sacredness is of course a negative quantity; it is a pretty domestic scene, masquerading as a Nativity.

Above it, 1135, is a Luini, Herodias's daughter receiving the head of John the Baptist. The princess's face is fine and characteristic, but the work as a whole does not adequately represent Luini at his best. It is cold and laboured.

The next room, that of the Maestri Diversi Italiani, contains small pictures of the later period, mostly of diminished interest. Amongst them, however, are some fine works. Number 1025, a beautiful and delicately finished little Mantegna, should be closely noticed. Its background is glorious. Number 1165, a rather pretty infant Christ lying on the Cross, by Allori, has a certain sentimental interest. I will allow the reader to make his own selection among these minor works. An Annunciation, by Garofalo, 1138, may be instructively compared with earlier and better treatments. Most of these pictures, indeed, are chiefly interesting as showing how later painters did ill what earlier artists had done much better. They are studies in decadence.

CHAPTER V.

THE HALLS OF THE FOREIGN SCHOOLS AND THE FIRST HALL OF THE VENETIAN SCHOOL.

THE next room, devoted to the Dutch School, contains several admirable works, some of which are of the first importance. Such are: 972, by Metzu; 870, by Heemskerck; 905, by Van der Werf; 854, by Mieris; 926, by Gerard Dou, etc. These works, however, have no natural organic connection with Florence, and though in many cases extremely beautiful and wonderfully finished, they seldom require any explanation. They do not therefore fall within the scope of this work, and I will leave them to the reader's native appreciation.

Somewhat the same may be said of the next room, containing Flemish and German pictures, many of which, however, are in their subjects more cognate with early Italian painting, so that they may often be compared to advantage with their southern compeers. In this room you cannot afford to overlook * 780 and * 801, two exquisite portraits by Memling. Number * 778 is a lovely portrait by the same, of a Benedictine monk in the character of St. Benedict — a frequent little excuse for portraiture. Number * 777 is a fine head of St. Philip by Dürer. Numbers 771 and 773 are good miniatures of saints by Poelemburg. Number 768 is a companion picture of St. James by Dürer. Number ** 769 is an unspeakably beautiful portrait by Memling, which, as an example of Flemish style, may be compared with ** 766, Dürer's essentially German portrait of his father, marvellous in its fidelity. Number 838 is a rather coarse portrait of Luther by Cranach; number 847, by the same, of Melancthon. Number 845 represents the Electors of Saxony. Number 765, ** Holbein's magnificent portrait of Richard Southwell, is too frank to be flattering — immensely superior to the one in the Louvre. Number 795 is * Roger van der Weyden's wonderful Deposition, where the characteristics of northern art may be well contrasted with Italian treatments of the same subject. The two elder saints are Joseph of Arimathea and Nicodemus. Number

784 is a fine portrait by Anthony Mor. I do not dwell on any of these, as not essential to Florence: but if you have time to see them, after seeing all that is distinctively local, they will well repay you for your trouble.

The Scuola Fiamminga e Tedesca, Prima Sala, similarly contains a number of admirable Flemish and German works. Conspicuous among these, on the wall which faces you as you enter, near the window, is ** Memling's exquisite Enthroned Madonna, where Our Lady's face is (as usual with Flemish art) somewhat vague and wooden, — a convention too sacred for art to tamper with, — while the two angels, especially the one with the apple to the left, are absolutely charming. The exquisite finish of everything in this triumph of Flemish painting should be carefully noted: the architecture of the arches, the children holding festoons of fruit and flowers (themselves most daintily and delicately finished), the delicious clear-cut landscape background, the richly wrought brocade behind Our Lady's back, her hair and robe, the carpet at her feet, the draperies of the angels, and the lovely ecclesiastical vestments worn by the apple-bearer, all deserve the closest study. This glorious picture glows like a jewel. Only the fact that it is not Italian hurries me away from it. But did not Mantegna take occasional hints from such festoons as these in contemporary Flemish painters?

Close by is a lovely * Van der Goes (or Aldegrever?) of the Madonna and Child, with St. Catherine and St. Barbara (?) and angels holding a crown above her head. Though inferior both in feeling and finish to the exquisite Madonna of the Portinari family, by the same artist, at Santa Maria Nuova (which go and see), it is nevertheless a splendid example of minute Flemish workmanship. I will only direct attention to the hair and robe of the Madonna and the architectural enrichments.

Other pictures on the same wall, well deserving study, are Kulmbach's (or Schauffelein's) Crucifixion of St. Peter and Conversion of St. Paul; an Adoration of the Magi, by an unknown fifteenth century Fleming (Gerard David? I think not); and some good little genre works by either Teniers.

Beyond the door is a charming portrait by Joost Van Cleef (Justus of Ghent), of a Dominican nun, in the character of the Mater Dolorosa. An Adam and Eve, by Floris, show once more the harsh northern conception of the nude, now largely modified by Italian example.

The end wall has a curious triptych by Nicolas Froment, the painter patronised by King René of Anjou (and the Meister Korn of the Germans). In the centre is the Resurrection of Lazarus, with the ghastly expression of returning life on a dead man's face rendered with painful truth and weird imagination. The bystanders holding their noses are conventional: see the old picture in the Belle Arti. The painting of their robes is very characteristic. The text of the left panel is, "Lord, if Thou hadst been here our brother had not died;" the subject of the right panel, the Magdalen anointing the feet of Christ. The Pharisee in this and the central picture seems to me most typically German: but there are also undeniably old French touches. Lafenestre claims it as French. Observe all the details. On the flaps outside in grisaille, are, on the left, Madonna and Child; on the right, the donors kneeling; dated 1461. Other good pictures on this wall I cannot particularise.

On the left wall, 731 is attributed to Jan Van Eyck (I think erroneously: it is probably

Foreign and Venetian Schools. 69

Dutch), * Adoration of the Magi. Very interesting for comparison both with the Italians and the Dürer. Notice the Moorish king, the architecture of the background, and the shepherds on the right flap. The Old King seems almost worthy of the great master: perhaps copied.

Below, 749, are two admirable portraits attributed to Petrus Cristus.

Here again I leave many fine works unnoticed, because of their want of connection with Florentine art or history.

For the same reason I will not notice any of the works of the French School just beyond, though Clouet's François Ier, Watteau's (?) Fluteplayer, and several others are well worth attention.

Now, pass out of this suite of rooms into the end corridor. The door to the left leads to a room containing the gems, many of which are worth close inspection. The corridor is chiefly occupied with sculpture, though it has also a few tolerable pictures. Cross it to the right, observing as you go the charming views out of all the windows, especially the end one looking down the Arno. Then, turn along the second long corridor, on the west side, and enter the first door to your left, which gives access to the Scuola Veneta, Sala Prima.

This room is full of good works (chiefly bought by Cardinal Leopoldo de' Medici from a Florentine merchant at Venice), which excellently exhibit the splendid Venetian colouring. They are not, however, of the first importance, nor does the Uffizi contain a sufficient number of examples to enable you to form a conception of the Venetian School, especially if you have not yet visited Venice. (The Pitti supplements it.)

On the entrance wall, to the left of the door as you enter, notice 585, Pordenone's fine Portrait of a Venetian Gentleman, well thrown up against a screen of wall, with admirable colour and accessories.

Near it, 604, is Carletto Veronese (son of Paolo), the Madonna in the clouds of glory, with St. Mary Magdalen, St. Justina, San Frediano of Lucca, with his rake, etc., a picture very characteristic of the later debased taste of Venice. The Magdalen has the face and costume of a courtesan.

Number 577 is a good portrait by Paris Bordone; 587, a much finer portrait by the same.

TITIAN. — FLORA.

Above it, 601, is a good characteristic portrait by Tintoretto of a Venetian admiral, where his peculiar tone of red is well marked.

On the left wall, 595, is a group of the painter's family, by Jacopo Bassano, also very typical of the later Venetian feeling.

Numbers **605 and *599 are portraits by Titian of the Duke and Duchess of Urbino, admirable as works of art, the painting of the armour and robes most noteworthy, but the duchess's face extremely unpleasing. The duke's is finely and boldly rendered.

Above, 596, is a Paolo Veronese, Esther brought before Ahasuerus. The central figures, the architecture, the accessories, and the spectators of this good work are all extremely characteristic of Veronese's manner. The whole is envisaged as a Venetian pageant of his time, with high-born Venetian ladies and great signiors of the period. Note the man in armour on the extreme left, with the more commonplace figure who balances him on the right. Colour and composition are well worth study as typical of the painter.

On an easel close by, 626, is *Titian's Flora, a characteristic example of large, idealised, voluptuous, aristocratic, Venetian womanhood; a fine model, excellently rendered. Hair, arms, and robe are all admirably painted. Note the dainty hands, with shade behind them, and the beautiful treatment of the left shoulder. The delicate flesh-tints could hardly be surpassed. The whole work is most light and luminous. The colour of the robe on the right is lovely.

Number 594 is a murky Domenico Tintoretto of an apparition of St. Augustine; below it is a characteristic Jacopo Bassano, Moses and the Burning Bush: both good examples of late Venetian manner.

On the end wall, 3388, is Tintoretto's Leda, a last product of the type initiated by Giorgione, and handed on by Titian. A graceful enough treatment of the nude, exquisite in its blended colour, less voluptuous and more ideal than Titian's models. The light and shade are marvellous. Notice the hands and feet, and the curtain in the background. The attendant by the chest is painted in one of Tintoretto's peculiar attitudes.

Below it, 571, attributed to Giorgione, perhaps by Caroto (or Torbido), is a noble * por-

MANTEGNA. — ADORATION OF THE MAGI (CENTRAL PANEL OF THE TRIPTYCH).

trait, said to be Gattamelata, where face, hair, armour, and everything are exquisitely painted.

Next it, ** 1111, is a marvellous triptych by Mantegna. One of the minutest and finest works of the great master's early period. Its finish is exquisite. Note the influence of northern art in it. The central panel, slightly curved, consists of an Adoration of the Magi, where the face of the Madonna and the treatment of the Child are highly typical of Mantegna's manner. The tall bent St. Joseph, the realistic portrait-like faces of the Three Kings (almost German or Flemish in tone), the camels and cortège in the background, the cave behind, and the still half conventional rocks, should all be noted. Observe, too, how in North Italian art intercourse with the East (through Venice) makes the cavalcade of the Kings really oriental in costume and features. All the faces in the background are fine studies of Asiatic or African types. This is a picture to look into and dwell upon. To the left is the Resurrection, where the straining upward faces and necks show Mantegna's love of setting himself difficulties to conquer. Each of these attitudes and faces deserves close study. To the right, the

Circumcision, where the shrinking boy in the Madonna's arms, and the aged figures close by, are thoroughly Mantegnesque. Observe the typical Paduan enrichment of the architectural background, and the Venetian touch in the bystander child sucking his finger. Every part of this magnificent work demands close attention. I have treated of it more fully in one of my articles in the *Pall-Mall Magazine*.

Number 648 is Titian's pretty portrait of Caterina Cornaro, Queen of Cyprus, in the character of St. Catherine, whose spiked wheel just appears in the background. There is nothing else saintly about this attractive portrait of a lovely and richly dressed Venetian woman. The purple satin of her sleeves, the rich green brocade, the jewelry and gewgaws, and the regal head-dress, are admirably painted. Notice especially the pearls, each produced by a few consummate touches. Note how art has become conscious and triumphant: it does things now with a twist of the hand which earlier it elaborated with endless minuteness.

Beyond the door, 586, is a noble portrait by Moroni: fine in attitude, expression, and detachment from its background.

On the right wall, 631, is a Giovanni Bellini; the Madonna by the Lake, a curious and unusual mystic attempt on this great painter's part to introduce novelty and variety into the groups of saints attendant on Our Lady. He had an order for so many, and he tried to vivify their grouping. To the extreme left is the Madonna enthroned, *without* the infant Saviour. (I cannot account for this unusual omission, was it for a mother who had lost her baby?) Beside her kneels St. Catherine of Alexandria, crowned; to the left, a most unconventional Catherine of Siena (?). Behind the parapet stand St. Peter and St. Paul, the former only recognisable by the type of his features. Below, children are playing with fruit and with a symbolical tree, perhaps that of the future Cross. As the figures have no haloes it is impossible to decide which is intended for the infant Saviour, but I take him to be the one playing with the tree, a natural symbol. To the extreme right are the two great plague-saints, St. Job, the patriarch (almost peculiar to the Adriatic, and well seen in Bellini's great plague-picture from San Giobbe now in the Academy at Venice), and St. Sebastian, pierced with arrows, proving this work to be most likely a votive plague-picture. In the background are other curious episodes, St. Anthony the Hermit with the Satyr, etc. The landscape, with its artificial rocks, is peculiar and poetical; it should be compared with Mantegna, Bellini's fellow pupil and brother-in-law. But I half doubt the ascription. This strangely mystic picture is, if authentic, unique among Bellini's works; whoever painted it, it represents an abortive attempt at that freer style of Sacra Conversazione which was later achieved in another form by Titian and his successors. (Some authorities attribute this work to Basaiti.)

Above it, *584 and *584 bis, are two good pictures by Cima da Conegliano, exhibiting well the Bellinesque type of Venetian Madonna, with her serene and queenly features, her strong column-like neck, and her peculiar head-dress. Notice the naked children, and the painting of the hands. The St. Peter with the keys is highly characteristic of Venetian treatment. This type of Madonna, best seen in Bellini at Venice, develops at last into Titian's ideal. Its evolution is interesting. The round-faced, strong-necked, matronly Venetian Madonna, extremely unlike any other Italian representation of Our Lady, seems to be ultimately derived from the school of Cologne, through Giovanni da Allemagna, a Rhenish artist who settled at Venice, and founded the school of the Vivarini. His type, altered and beautified by Bellini, was further modified by Titian and his successors, but always retained at Venice its matronly roundness and its fine neck. Elsewhere in Italy the Madonna, derived directly from the thin-faced fretful Byzantine type, is slight and girlish, no matter how varied in other particulars.

Number *583 bis is a fragmentary Carpaccio, of some Old Testament subject (or of a Way to Calvary), where all the figures are most typical of their painter.

Number 579 is an Annunciation of the school of Paolo Veronese. (Morelli attributes it to Zelotti.) The Madonna is one of Veronese's Venetian models. The action takes place in a vast loggia, of the school of Sansovino, where only the formal arrangement reminds one of the empty central colonnade in Neri di Bicci's pictures. The Announcing Angel, with his annunciation lily in his hand, just descended from the sky, and raising his hand with a theatrical gesture, contrasts in every respect with earlier and more sacred treatments. He is just a plump Venetian figure, ostentatiously posing himself in what he considers a telling attitude. It is interesting to note here the retention of all the formal features, such as the garden in the background, the prie-dieu, etc., side by side with the utter and lamentable transformation in the spirit of the scene. Note the Holy Ghost, descending in the midst in a vague glory of cherubs. You cannot properly understand such pictures as these unless you have first studied earlier representations of the same subjects.

Number 592, by Sebastiano del Piombo, represents the Death of Adonis, a Renaissance mythological subject, treated in Sebastiano's earlier manner, almost wholly Venetian, but with tinges of Roman influence beginning to show in it.

Just beyond, 578, is a pleasing portrait by Paris Bordone.

Number 575 is Lorenzo Lotto's Holy Family, with St. Anne and the Madonna in a familiar attitude (we have seen it before), and St. James and St. Jerome introduced in the background. It should be compared with the pair by Cima, close by, to show the development in Venetian treatments of this subject.

Number 574, by Polidoro Veneziano, is the Madonna and Child with St. Francis, where the composition and the landscape background are in the style initiated by Titian.

On the entrance wall, again, is 572, Paolo Veronese's St. Catherine, the exact analogue of the Annunciation just noticed.

Below it, 627 is attributed to Sebastiano del Piombo (probably Dosso Dossi). Striking portrait of a general.

CHAPTER VI.

THE SECOND HALL OF THE VENETIAN SCHOOL AND THE EARLY FLORENTINE PAINTINGS.

THE next room, the second hall of the Venetian School, has, left of the door, 590, a Madonna and Child with St. John, by Titian, in a mandorla of cherubs. A good picture in a transitional manner.

Near it is 609, reduced copy of Titian's celebrated Battle of Cadore (burnt in the fire at the Doge's Palace in 1577), a work noted for its life and movement, and its vigorous treatment.

Number 3390 is a Tintoretto, one of his finest portraits, full of character and dignity, and admirable in colour.

Number 613 is a fine luminous portrait by Paris Bordone.

The left wall has a fine portrait of Sansovino the sculptor, by Tintoretto; 636, a Crucifixion, by Paolo Veronese, well exhibiting the later non-sacred conception of this subject; and *633, a

Early Florentine Paintings.

beautiful Madonna and Child, with the boy Baptist and St. Anthony the Hermit, by Titian. The last is one of his most exquisite Madonnas. Above it is an admirable cartoon by Bellini (or of his school) for a Pietà.

On the end wall, 623, is a fine Holy Family with St. Mary Magdalen, by Palma Vecchio (perhaps a copy), in which the face and head-dress of the Madonna, and the face and hair of the Magdalen, should be carefully compared with Cima and Titian. The colour is rich and well harmonised.

Beneath it, 639, is a fine portrait of a Man with a Guitar by an unknown artist (Moretto?).

Number 625 exhibits Titian's most mundane style of Madonna, with a well-made Venetian young lady in the character of St. Catherine. The infant Christ has here attained the furthest height of Renaissance treatment, while Our Lady's face is frankly human and ladylike. Trace its evolution by the aid of the Palma above it, the Bellini, the Cima, etc.

Number * 630 is Giorgione's Judgment of Solomon, with fine landscape background and striking figures. This and its companion piece are among the very few works attributed to this great Master which Morelli allows to be authentic. They were probably painted in his seventeenth or eighteenth year. The deep colour, the sparkling touch, the feeling for nature, and the fine drawing of the figure are there already.

Number 589, Paolo Veronese's Martyrdom of St. Justina, shows a Venetian lady, pallid from fear, with Moors and negroes as bystanders or executioners, and portraits of Venetian gentlemen as Roman officials, afraid of getting their fine robes spoiled by the spurting blood of the martyr. A most frank instance of a sacred subject distorted from its purpose, but pleasing in colour and large in treatment. Nice architecture.

Above it is 628, Bonifazio's Last Supper.

Number * 621 is a Giorgione, the Child Moses undergoing the ordeal of fire — a legendary subject. Compare with the companion piece.

Number ** 622, also by Giorgione, is a splendid portrait of a Knight of Malta: a noble and authentic work, very much repainted.

Number 642 is a good portrait by Moroni.

On the right wall is 619, Palma Vecchio's * Judith, which strikes a key-note. It is very much injured. Also, notice 618, an unfinished Madonna and Child, by Titian, a copy of his

Early Florentine Paintings.

famous Pesaro Madonna at Venice; 617, Tintoretto's Marriage at Cana, a sketch for the great picture at Venice, with alterations; and, on the same wall, several good portraits.

On the entrance wall, by the door, is a Transfiguration by Savoldo, with the curious modern touch and tendency of that very original Lombard painter. Note the transformation of earlier conceptions. Above it, 646, is Tintoretto's Sacrifice of Isaac.

I do not enlarge upon many of these pictures, because the Venetian school is so much better studied in Venice than at Florence, where the series is but fragmentary. Those who have visited Venice will be able to put most of these works into their proper order in the evolution of Venetian painting. For those who have not, they must remain unplaced till another visit.

Return to the second Long Corridor, and take the first door to the left, which leads through a passage (with portraits of painters) to the Sala di Lorenzo Monaco. This room contains some of the finest and most interesting works of the Early Florentine period. Left of the door, as you enter, is *1310, a Gentile da

Fabriano: four isolated saints, portions of an altar-piece, with the Madonna (who once was there) omitted. On the left is St. Mary Magdalen, with her alabaster box of ointment; next to her St. Nicholas of Bari, with his golden balls: on his robes are embroidered the Nativity, the Adoration of the Magi, the Flight into Egypt, the Massacre of the Innocents, the Presentation in the Temple, and the Baptism of Christ. Note such subjects hereafter, embroidered on the robes of other bishops. They often throw light on the personages represented. Then, St. John the Baptist of Florence, as the ascetic saint, and St. George, with the red cross on his lance and shield, a striking figure. In the *cuspidi* above, other saints and angels. This picture comes from the church of St. Nicholas in Florence, and the Nicholas stood on the right hand of Our Lady.

Number 1302, beneath, is a predella by Benozzo Gozzolo: (1) Marriage of St. Catherine of Alexandria, a charming girlish figure; (2) Pietà with St. John and the Magdalen; (3) St. Anthony with his crutch and book, and St. Benedict holding a book and arrow. This is from Santa Croce.

Early Florentine Paintings. 85

On the end wall, ** 1309, by Don Lorenzo Monaco, is a great altar-piece of the Coronation of the Virgin, in a magnificent tabernacle of three arches. Adequately to describe this noble picture, the only important work now remaining by Fra Angelico's master, would require many pages. I note a few points. Below are the circles of heaven, with stars and angels. The centre once held a reliquary, now gone, about which angels swing censers.

In the group of saints under the left arch, nearest the throne, is St. John the Baptist of Florence; then, St. Peter with the keys, and St. Benedict, with a scourge (this being a Camaldolese-Benedictine picture, painted for Don Lorenzo's own monastery of the Angeli at Florence; above him St. Stephen, with the stones on his head; beside whom stands St. Paul, holding his sword and his Epistle to the Romans; then, St. James the Greater with a staff, St. Anthony Abbot with a crutch, and other saints less discernible, among whom I believe I detect St. Louis of France, and St. Louis of Toulouse. In the opposite arch: on the extreme right, to balance St. Benedict, in white robes, is St. Romuald, founder of the Camaldolese order (a branch of the Benedictines); next him, St. Andrew and St. John the Evangelist; behind the last, St. Lawrence, with his gridiron (Lorenzo's name saint); St. Bartholomew with his knife, and St. Francis with his Franciscan robes and crucifix. Between the last two, a bishop, probably San Zanobi, as his mitre bears the Florentine lily. Between him and St. Francis is, I think, St. Vincent. The rest I cannot decipher. Observe the numerous angels, representing the monastery. In the *cuspidi*, an Annunciation, and Christ blessing. Many of the figures on the frame may also be identified. On the left are King David, Noah with the ark, and other Old Testament characters; on the right, Daniel, Moses with the stone tables, and various prophets. The predella contains Bible scenes, and stories from the life of St. Benedict. The first represents his death, where his disciple St. Maurus sees his soul ascending to heaven; the second, his teaching in his monastery, with St. Maurus and the young monk who was tempted by the devil. (See the same subject in the very different St. Benedict series by Francesco di Giorgio Martini in the Scuola Toscana, Terza Sala.) The third is a Nativity, and the fourth an Adoration of the Magi; the fifth represents St. Benedict in his cell with Benedictine saints, male and female: he sends out St. Maurus to rescue St. Placidus from drowning; the sixth shows the resuscitation of a novice, killed by a falling house at the Convent of Monte-Cassino. (The same scenes occur, with others, in Spinello Aretino's frescoes in the Sacristy at San Miniato.) Taking it all round, it is a noble work for its date, worth close study.

Number 1305 is a Domenico Veneziano, representing the Madonna and Child, enthroned, under a very peculiar canopy, with St. John the Baptist, St. Francis (Bernard?), San Zanobi, and St. Lucy. (It was painted for the church of St. Lucy at Florence.) A hard picture, in very peculiar colouring, but with fine drawing and good characterisation. It is, in point of fact, an early attempt at oil-painting, the secret of which Domenico had learnt, and which he imparted to Andrea del Castagno, who murdered him in order that he alone might possess it. The colouring is clear and bright, but lacks harmony; it is anything but melting. The drawing and composition remind one of Andrea del Castagno.

Number 24, by Lorenzo di Credi, is a Virgin adoring the Child. The infant is exquisite.

Number 1286, ** Botticelli's Adoration of the Magi, is one of the painter's finest sacred works, where all the conventional elements are retained, while a totally new meaning is given to the merest detail, such as the great ruined classical temple, and far more to the group of attendants on the Three Kings, all of whom are contemporary Florentine portraits. Notice in the figure of the Young King, to the right, in white (a portrait of Lorenzo de' Medici), how completely Botticelli has transformed and spiritualised the earlier conception. The portrait faces of all the Three Kings, indeed, are exquisitely beautiful: the eldest, seen in profile, is Cosimo Pater Patriæ. Equally fine is the group of men of letters and statesmen to the right. Do not overlook the poetical Botticellian touch in the light gauze veil thrown over the Second King's gift, nor the fur on his dress, nor the dainty painting of the peacock on the ruin, nor the thoughtful face of the draped figure in yellow, to the extreme right, nor the haughty aristocratic mouths of the Medici to the left, nor indeed anything about this wonderful picture.

BOTTICELLI — ADORATION OF THE MAGI.

Every face is significant, every fold of the drapery is beautiful and flowing. (From Santa Maria Novella.)

Number 1297 is *Ghirlandajo's beautiful Madonna and Child, with adoring Angels, a work of his early manner. All the details of this picture are marvellous. Observe the architecture and decoration of the canopy, and the trees in the background. Also, the carpet on the steps, and the vase of flowers, including Florentine lilies. One stage below the Madonna stand the two archangels, Michael with his sword, and the half-womanish Raphael with the box of ointment he carried to Tobit, — both exquisite figures in Ghirlandajo's most attractive manner. A step lower down kneel two sainted bishops; to the right, San Zanobi, with the lily on his morse, to the left another, who is probably St. Just, because the picture comes from the church of San Giusto, near Florence. Note the figures on their robes. This is one of Ghirlandajo's best and most carefully painted panels.

Number 17 is *Fra Angelico's famous tabernacle of the Madonna and Child, with St. John the Baptist and St. Mark the Evangelist, patrons of Florence and of the Convent of San Marco.

This is an early picture (1433), the drawing still very crude and rigid. It has a draped and somewhat vapid infant, Giottesque in type, and its Madonna disappoints; but round its frame are charming angels, continually copied. On the outside of the flaps, St. Peter and St. Mark again (or is it St. Jerome?) with the lion. Beneath it, 1294, its predella, relating to these same saints. In the left compartment, St. Peter preaches at Rome, while St. Mark the Evangelist takes down his words to write his gospel. Centre, Adoration of the Magi, where the action of one of the Kings and Joseph is very unusual. In the right compartment is the Martyrdom of St. Mark, who is dragged by a rope at Alexandria, with the overthrow of his assailants by hail and lightning: in the background, Christ appearing to him in prison. This was painted for the Guild of Linen Merchants, whose patron was St. Mark.

On the right-hand wall, 39, is ** Botticelli's exquisite Birth of Venus, one of the most lovely embodiments of Renaissance feeling. It was painted, like the Primavera, which it closely resembles in tone and feeling, for Lorenzo de' Medici's villa at Castello. In the centre, Venus

BOTTICELLI. — BIRTH OF VENUS (DETAIL).

rises nude from a foaming sea, throned on a scallop shell. Her figure has a strange elusive beauty. Her long fair hair, her wistful face, her lithe ideal form, are wholly Botticellian. The picture, though pagan, is anything but classical: it has modern pessimism in it. As a Tuscan embodiment of the nude, again, compare this unspeakably graceful form with Lorenzo di Credi's merely human Venus in the Sala Seconda Toscana. The paleness of the flesh-tints only enhances the ideal feeling of the work. To the left, figures resembling the March and April of the Primavera scatter flowers around the goddess. To the right, a draped form, like the May of the Primavera, prepares to throw a brocaded mantle over Venus's shoulders. All the figures and draperies are instinct with Botticelli's peculiar flowing movement. This is a picture to linger before for hours. It embodies better than any other the pagan side of this earnest painter's nature. Yet its paganism is superficial: the ascetic ideal, the profound moral yearning, are everywhere apparent.

The pictures in the remaining rooms, though in many cases valuable and interesting, do not call for explanation. The next halls to the left, as you continue along the corridor, are devoted to portraits of painters (or what pass for such), chiefly by themselves, but in several instances of doubly doubtful authenticity — that is to say, it is not always certain that they are really the work of the artists whose names they bear, nor again that they represent the person they are said to portray. Among the most important (with this needful reservation) are Raphael, Perugino, Cranach, Holbein the Younger, Van der Helst, Van Dyck, Titian, and Rubens. Of later painters, the most often noticed is the charming if somewhat coquettish Mme. le Brun, familiar from copies; the most noteworthy are Angelica Kaufmann, Ingres, Jules Breton, Watts, Millais, Puvis de Chavannes, Leighton, and Cabanel. The Hall of Baroccio, beyond, contains numerous good pictures of the seventeenth and eighteenth centuries, among which you may note fine works by Bronzino, Rubens, Guido, Velasquez, etc., outside the range of this guide. At the end of the corridor are three rooms containing a magnificent collection of drawings by the great artists. Students of Morelli will know how to value these — but I do not presume to write for students of Morelli.

CHAPTER VII.

THE SCULPTURE IN THE UFFIZI.

THE sculpture in the Uffizi, being almost entirely classical in origin, forms a subject of special study, outside the author's sphere, and scarcely possible of treatment within the narrow limits which can be given to it in this Guide. Those who wish to pursue it seriously should read the different questions up in Gardner's "Handbook" or Murray's "History of Sculpture," or else in Lübke or Fürtwangler. Moreover, most of the antiques in the Uffizi were freely restored and even rudely modernised during the sixteenth and seventeenth centuries, before the sanctity of an ancient work was thoroughly recognised. Many of them have, therefore, modern heads and arms. Others are provided with antique heads, which, however, do not always belong to them, violence having been done to neck and torso in order to effect an apparently natural junction. In origin, most of the statues and busts are Roman, or were found at Rome: they were brought here from the Villa Medici on the Pincian Hill by Leopoldo de' Medici in 1779. They have thus no organic connection with Florence. Nevertheless, I give a brief and quite unauthoritative account here of the most important works, leaving the reader to follow up the subject if he will in more specialist treatises. A good little book on plastic art in general is Marquand and Frothingham's "History of Sculpture."

On the staircase, last landing, to the left is Silenus with the infant Bacchus, in bronze, a Renaissance copy of the antique original at the Villa Pinciana at Rome. The same subject in marble exists in the Louvre. To the right is a bronze statue of Mars. Round them are portrait busts of the Medici, Apollo, etc.

On the entrance landing, 18, is a horse, rearing, supposed to belong to the group of Niobe (see later); 24, 25 are two Molossian dogs; 19, a celebrated *boar, of Greek workmanship, one of the finest specimens of antique animal sculpture. There is a good bronze copy by Pietro Tacca in the Mercato Nuovo. Behind it, and opposite, are triumphal pillars; in the niches, Hadrian, Trajan, Augustus, and other Roman portrait statues.

Enter the Long Corridor, and turn to the right. At the end, 38 represents Hercules and the Centaur Nessus. Almost the entire figure of the Hercules is of Renaissance workmanship. So are the head and arms of the Centaur (restored by Giovanni da Bologna). The antique portion, however, is of very fine workmanship.

Near the left wall, 39, is a * fine Roman sarcophagus, representing the life of the person whose body it contained, from infancy to old age. I give some account of the reliefs, as a specimen. (If the subject interests you, follow up the other sarcophagi with the official guide.) On the right end, in the left portion, is the birth of the subject, represented as a child, with his mother and nurse. In the right portion is his education; he reads a book with his tutor, while above are the Muses, — the tragic Muse, as representing poetry; another, holding a scroll, for history; and a third, Urania, with globe and compasses, for mathematics and astronomy. (The official catalogue refers the last, I think less justly, to the tracing of the subject's horoscope.) On the face of the sarcophagus, to the right, is his marriage, Hymen holding the torch, and Juno bringing husband and wife together. (The features of the bride would lead one to suppose that he married his grandmother, unless this figure is rather to be recognised as the bride's mother, with the bride to the right behind her, which the veil makes improbable.) The arrangement highly foreshadows the mediæval Sposalizio. In the centre, the hero, whose features have now the character of a portrait, offers a sacrifice before setting out on a warlike expedition; he is throwing incense on an altar, while an attendant smites a bull, and a boy plays a double flute beside him; in the background is a temple. On the left, as conqueror, in a military cloak, attended by Victory with a palm, he shows mercy to the women and children of the vanquished. On the left end, he is represented hunting, and, farther to the left, as in retirement in old age, now a bearded man, seated on a magisterial chair, while attendants remove his greaves and the rest of his armour, signifying a return from military to civic life. The whole design is very spirited. The running together of the separate scenes, without formal

The Sculpture in the Uffizi. 97

dividing lines, is highly characteristic of antique reliefs.

On the right wall, opposite, are 45 and * 47, busts of Julius and Augustus; several others about. Compare them for age and evolution of features.

On the left wall, right and left of door, are two more busts of Augustus. Note the features.

On the right wall is 44, statue of Attis, erroneously restored as a barbaric king. The head is modern. 37 represents Pompeius.

On the left wall, to the right and left of the door, are 46, * a fine bust of Livia, wife of Tiberius; 48, ** Marcus Agrippa, builder of the Pantheon, with powerful reserved Etruscan features; 52, an athlete. Beside it, 51, Pan and Olympus, the latter modern. Then, right and left, busts, of which 60 is a charming boy, * Britannicus. 56 is a sarcophagus with Phædra and Hippolytus on the left: on the right, Hippolytus hunting the boar; in two compartments. To the left is 59, an athlete, with vase; to the right, 58, a wingless Victory, with palm and wreath; to the right is 62, a sarcophagus, with the Rape of the Leucippidæ by Castor and Pollux.

The busts which succeed are sufficiently named on the pedestals for the passing visitor. On the left is 67, an athlete — note the numerous variants; on the right, 66, a faun, wrongly restored as a Bacchus; beyond it, 68, a sarcophagus with the labours of Hercules on the face, the Nemean lion, hydra, boar, stag, Augean stables, etc. Notice on the right, 77, the foppish head of * Otho, with his frizzed wig, a fine piece of handicraft; on the left, good busts of Nero, Caligula, and Galba. Right and left, 74 and 75, are, respectively, Pomona and an athlete. (Notice replicas.) On the left is 78, a sarcophagus with Tritons and Nereids, accompanied by Cupids. In 85 and others notice the curious Roman head-dresses. No. 71 is a charming baby Nero. 81 and 82 are Urania and Ariadne. Note, as we pass here from the Julian and Claudian Cæsars to the later emperors, the sudden loss of aristocratic dignity, now replaced by the coarse and vulgar features of Vitellius, or the mere bourgeois capacity of * Vespasian. Even Titus, though better, has not the fine type of the patrician emperors.

On the right are 88, Ganymede with the eagle; contrast later at the Bargello with Cellini; 90, vestal, in the act of throwing incense; a nobly modest figure; 95, a sarcophagus representing the Calydonian boar, with the huntress Atalanta: heads mostly modern. This boar should be compared with the one on the staircase. The story is confused; read up in any book of reference under head, Meleager. Near the door of the Tribuna, much restored Muse, and good Hercules resting on his club. To the right and left of the door are two stages in the evolution of * Trajan.

Enter the Tribuna, which contains five celebrated statues, originally selected as the finest of the collection. As with the pictures, however, the choice reflects rather the taste of the beginning of this century than that of its end. These works are not in themselves of the first æsthetic importance, and many of them have been restored out of all recognition. Their vogue belonged to a day before the discovery of the finest Greek originals. The first is a * Satyr playing on the cymbal, and pressing the *krupezion* with his feet. Only the torso is antique. The clever head and face, the arms, and part of the feet were restored by a Renaissance sculptor, probably Michael Angelo. The expression is entirely that of Renaissance Italy, not of classical sculpture. The original has been doubtfully referred to the School of Praxiteles. The second, * the Wrestlers, is believed to be a work of the School of Polycleitus. The heads, though probably antique, belong to other statues (of the School of Scopas), and resemble those of the Children of Niobe. They are without expression, and their placidity is wholly out of accord with the action of the vigorous struggling bodies. Many parts of the limbs are modern, and have not been correctly restored in every instance. The third is * the famous and overrated Medici Venus, found in Hadrian's Villa at Tivoli in 1680. The unpleasing pose of the left hand and of the right arm is due to the restorer. An inscription on the base (modern, but said to reproduce the original one) gives the authorship to one Cleomenes, of Athens. A sculptor of that name worked at Rome in the age of Augustus. The fourth is * the so-called Arrotino, a Scythian grinding his knife to flay Marsyas. The subject has been discovered by means of bas-reliefs and medals. The fifth is * the young Apollo, said to be wholly antique. It is probably a copy

TRIBUNA (UFFIZI GALLERY).

from an original by Praxiteles, and is supposed to be the handicraft of the same sculptor as the Medici Venus.

Return to the Long Corridor. On the left is another sarcophagus with the labours of Hercules. Compare with the previous one. To the right and left are a Polyhymnia and a Mercury; beside the latter, two stages in the evolution of Hadrian. To the right, 103, is a pleasing bust of Plotina, wife of Trajan; to the left, 110, a Bacchanalian scene (Triumph of Bacchus). The god, to the left, is drawn by a male and female centaur. In front, Ariadne is similarly drawn by panthers. Chained slaves precede them: mœnads and fauns accompany. To the right, 112, is a Venus and Cupid. Compare the Venus on the left, 113, in attitude, with the Medici. Beyond it is a sarcophagus with Cupids, and another with Triton and Nereids. At the end, right and left, are two Apollos.

In the Short Corridor are charming little Cupids, of which 123 is very pleasing; on the left, a Bacchante, with a panther. In the centre, * 36, seated Roman portrait statue; beyond, right and left, portrait busts of the Antonine period, betraying the faint beginnings of the Decadence. Number 133 is a Minerva, somewhat rigid in attitude: archaic or archaistic; on the left, 138, is the famous * Thorn-extractor, a graceful statue of a boy athlete: one of many copies.

In 136, etc., the various stages of Marcus Aurelius, the philosopher emperor, are interestingly indicated.

Number 141 is a beautiful candelabrum; 129 a sarcophagus with Phaethon falling into the Eridanus, represented by a river-god, close by, his sisters metamorphosed into poplars; 145, Venus stooping at the bath, a graceful small statue, like the famous one in the Vatican. The head is modern. On the left, 2, is a Mars, in basalt; opposite, 134, Venus with the sword. Number 35 is a ** magnificent seated portrait statue of a Roman lady, known as Agrippina. The pose and draperies are admirable.

In the second Long Corridor are busts of Emperors of the Decadence, continuously losing both in character and craftsmanship. Numbers 155 and 156 represent Marsyas, the first restored by Donatello; on the right, 162, a Nereid on a sea-horse, and 169, Discobolus, probably a copy of the famous work of Myron.

The Sculpture in the Uffizi.

In the room to the left, the Hall of Painters, is a fine antique marble vase of Greek workmanship, known as the Medici vase, and with admirable reliefs of the Sacrifice of Iphigeneia, who may be seen prostrate below the statue of Artemis on the side next the windows.

The next door to the left leads to the Hall of the Inscriptions, with numerous works of sculpture, many of them of inferior interest, but containing some masterpieces. To the right of the door is a pleasing * Venus Genetrix, covered with a light Coan robe. To the left, * a priestess, with exquisite drapery; and on altars to right and left, Venus Urania and * Mercury, the last very fine. In the centre, on an Egyptian base, is a beautiful group of * Bacchus and Ampelus. Round the walls are inscriptions and reliefs, interesting mostly to the scholar. Near the entrance into the next room, 283, is a figure with Oriental tinge, perhaps an Attis.

The room beyond, Hall of the Hermaphrodite, has, 318, a colossal head known as the * Dying Alexander, — in reality, a giant of the Pergamenian School. Round the walls are a series of ** fine reliefs of the Augustan period, from the altar of the Augustan Peace, erected by the great emperor in A. D. 12, on his final pacification of the Empire. They are sufficiently explained by their labels. These noble and graceful works exhibit the simple idealism of the age of Augustus. The one which represents the members of the Claudian family is particularly beautiful. In the centre of the room, 306, repetition of the favourite statue of the Hermaphrodite, the lower portion modern. Number 290 is a seated statue of Ceres; 316, an Antinous, not one of the most pleasing representations of the subject; 308, a Ganymede, so restored by Benvenuto Cellini as to be practically his own work. It would be beside my purpose to enter more fully into the contents of these rooms, but many of the sculptures (such as the superb head of Seneca or the colossal torso of a faun) deserve thorough examination at the hands of those who desire to understand classical sculpture.

In the Long Corridor, again, 186, is a wounded soldier, of the Pergamenian school.

The Hall of Niobe, to the left, farther on, contains seventeen groups or single figures of ** Niobe and her children, struck by the arrows

HALL OF NIOBE (UFFIZI GALLERY).

of Artemis (some of them duplicates). These are believed to be good Roman copies from the Greek originals of the School of Scopas. The faces and figures of all should be compared with those of the Melian Aphrodite (Venus of Milo), in the Louvre. They seem to have originally occupied the pediment of a temple, with the large standing figure of Niobe herself in the centre (placed here at the right hand end of the hall). The figure opposite is supposed to be that of their tutor or pedagogue. The other figures declined gradually in height from the centre on either side, and ended in prostrate forms, like the one opposite the middle window.

Enter the Long Corridor again. Here are more portrait busts of the Decadence, several good Roman altars with inscriptions, inferior statues, etc.; near the end, 236, fine sacrificial altar of the age of Augustus, dedicated to his Lares, with the date inscribed by means of the consular years — the thirteenth of Augustus, the first of M. Plautus Silvanus; and, at the end, an altered copy of the Laocoon, an antique in the Vatican at Rome, of the Rhodian School: this variant is by Baccio Bandinelli, who considered that he had improved upon the original. Later critics have not endorsed his opinion. But the original itself belongs to a late school of Greek sculpture which sacrificed plastic repose to violent action and dramatic movement.

CHAPTER VIII.

THE PITTI PALACE.

THIRD in importance among the collections of Florence must be reckoned that of the Pitti Palace. Indeed, it is probable that most people would even now regard it as first, or at least second, in rank, owing to the large number of masterpieces of the High Renaissance which it contains; but its comparative poverty in works of the increasingly popular masters of the Early Renaissance will doubtless make it take a less exalted place in the estimation of the coming generation.

The Palazzo in which it is housed is itself historical. Designed by Brunelleschi, the architect of the Cathedral dome, it was begun about 1440 for Luca Pitti, the head of the great house who formed at that date the chief rivals of the Medici. Luca conspired, however, in 1466 against Piero de' Medici (son of Cosimo **Pater**

Patriæ, and father of Lorenzo); and, his conspiracy failing, the building remained unfinished till 1549. It then came into the hands of the Medici; and Cosimo I., completing the central block, made it thenceforth his principal residence. It has ever since ranked as the chief Grand Ducal and Royal Palace in Florence. The existing building includes several additions to Brunelleschi's design, which will be pointed out as you stand before it.

Cross the picturesque Ponte Vecchio, with its jewellers' shops, topped by the connecting passage from the Uffizi, and continue along the straight street in front till you come on the left to a huge prison-like building, which crowns a slight eminence. That is the Pitti Palace. At first sight, you will probably find it just sombre and repulsive; after many visits, its massive masonry, its dignified architecture, its fine proportions will slowly grow upon you. The central portion alone, in three stories, represents Brunelleschi's work; notice the huge blocks of which it is built, true Etruscan in their solidity, only worked at the edge so as to give an increased effect of vastness and ruggedness. Originally, as in most other castle-like Florentine palaces,

PITTI PALACE.

there were no windows at all on the ground floor (save the little square openings above), and the façade must then have looked even gloomier than now; but under the Medici Grand Dukes, Bartolommeo Ammanati boldly introduced the round-arched windows below, — a feat which would seem almost impossible in so solid a building without endangering the stability of the entire superstructure. The wings in line with the centre were added in the seventeenth century; those at an angle to it, running out toward the street, not till the eighteenth.

The entrance to the Picture Gallery is in the wing to the left, through an unimposing doorway. Mount the shabby stairs, and pass through the still shabbier gallery passage into the too magnificent and gorgeously decorated suite of apartments.

We enter first the Hall of the Iliad. (The names written over the doors are those of the next rooms, to which they give access.) Here, more even than elsewhere, recollect that I do not pretend to dispense critical opinions.

To the left of the door, as you enter, 236, is a Bassano; Christ in the house of Mary and Martha; Lazarus carving. In this late Venetian picture, painted in the High Renaissance style, we have still a faint reminiscence of the traditional gesture of Martha, shown long before in the Giovanni da Milano at Santa Croce. Otherwise, the picture is a Venetian domestic interior of its date, largely painted for the sake of its buxom fair-haired Magdalen and its picturesque accessories. Observe the transformed cruciform halo.

Above it, * 235, is an excellent Holy Family by Rubens (probably a copy); of course frankly Flemish and sixteenth century. Note how the infant St. John of Florence with his lamb is now transferred to northern art through the influence of Raphael.

Number 232, by Sustermans, calls itself a Holy Family. In reality, it consists of good portraits of uninteresting contemporaries.

In number 233, Pontormo's St. Anthony is equally transformed from his earlier type.

Over the door is an affected, long-necked Madonna, with sprawling Child, by Parmigianino.

Beyond the door, * 229, is a good portrait of a lady in a red dress with green sleeves, known as La Gravida, and ascribed to Raphael. Above it, 228, half-length of Christ, by Titian, of his early period.

Number 225, * Andrea del Sarto's Assumption, is a noble example of his beautiful colouring. The Madonna in clouds, above, in a fine luminous glory, with her ring of baby angels, is a charming portrait of the artist's wife, Lucrezia, whom you will meet again in this gallery. Below, the Apostles look up in wonder: one gazes into the empty sarcophagus: there are just twelve of them. Conspicuous among them is St. Thomas, in a red and blue costume, by the steps of the sepulchre, holding up his hands with some surviving reminiscence of his earlier position, as if in expectation of the Sacra Cintola. (See the reliefs in the Cathedral and in Or San Michele, and the pictures in the Uffizi and Belle Arti.) In the foreground kneel two later spectator saints, — Nicholas of Bari, with his golden balls, and St. Margaret of Cortona, — whence it comes, — the Franciscan. Such a picture as this can only fully be understood by the light cast by earlier paintings.

Beyond again, 224, 223, 222, are three good portraits by Ridolfo Ghirlandajo; a Flemish artist (perhaps Quintin Matsys); and Bonifazio.

Over the next door is a Christ in a glory, with saints, by Annibale Carracci, very characteristic of this painter's composite manner. There are touches in it of Correggio and of many others.

Number 219, by Perugino, the Madonna adoring the Child, is a beautiful picture.

Number 216, a * Paolo Veronese, is a portrait of Daniele Barbaro.

On the end wall are several good portraits by Paolo Veronese, Titian, and others. In 214, Baroccio (a copy from Correggio), observe the complete transformation of the earlier conceptions of the Madonna and Child, St. Jerome and St. Catherine, and adoring angels. Number 212 is a good portrait of Cosimo I. by Bronzino.

Number 208, by Fra Bartolommeo, is a splendid and unusually pleasing example of his Enthroned Madonnas, with saints and angels. Our Lady sits under a canopy, most characteristic of this painter. The child Christ is placing a ring on the finger of St. Catherine of Siena. To the left, the most conspicuous figure is that of St. George, in attitude reminiscent of Donatello (often called St. Michael, but he bears a martyr's palm). To the right stands the painter's namesake, St. Bartholomew, with his knife. Among the other saints, one can vaguely recognise Dominic with his lily, St. Thomas Aquinas, and perhaps Santa Reparata of Florence, in red and green. The angels in the foreground are highly characteristic. So is the distribution of light and shade, and the varied composition.

Number 207, a fine portrait of a goldsmith, by Ridolfo Ghirlandajo, was formerly attributed to Leonardo — of whom it is quite worthy.

Over the door, 202, a Biliverti — subject, the angel receiving the gifts of Tobias and Tobit — is chiefly interesting as exhibiting the later theatrical manner.

Number 201, ** Titian's noble portrait of Cardinal Ippolito de' Medici, in Hungarian military costume, after his campaign against the Turks, is a study in red.

Above it, 200, is a copy (or replica?) of a portrait by Titian of Philip II. of Spain.

On the right wall, 199, is a Granacci, a Madonna and Child, with infant St. John, a good example of the later development of this Florentine subject.

Above it, 198, is a portrait by Velasquez; over the door, 196, a Paolo Veronese, St. Benedict and saints. Number 195, by Giacomo

Francia, is a portrait of a man, admirable in its simple severity and excellent painting.

Number 191, an Andrea del Sarto, is another Assumption of the Madonna, unfinished, closely resembling that opposite, and doubtless ordered on the strength of it. The two should be compared together. Note the similar position and costume of the St. Thomas, with his foot on the base of the sarcophagus. The kneeling saints in the foreground are, however, here two of the Apostles, and the background is different. The upward-straining faces of the spectators are full of reality. (One of the kneeling saints, in red cloak and blue vest, is Andrea's own portrait, in the character of St. Andrew.)

Number 190, by Sustermans, is an excellent portrait of a Prince of Denmark.

Over the door, 186, by Paolo Veronese, is a Baptism of Christ. We again observe the Venetian faces, and the complete transformation of earlier motives, such as the angel with the towel. Recollect what baptisms used to be in the fourteenth century. The pretty Venetian in the rear is meant for St. Catherine.

Near the window, 184, is Andrea del Sarto's fine portrait of himself, injured.

SEBASTIANO DEL PIOMBO. — MARTYRDOM OF ST. AGATHA.

Number 185, a ** Titian — an early work, attributed to Giorgione — represents a musical concert, with three fine portraits of men playing instruments, the middle one full of character, the hands and drapery especially admirable. The central head alone retains much of the primitive touch; the other two have been repainted with disastrous effect till all individuality is gone from them.

In 237, by Rosso Rossi, the total transformation of the traditional St. Sebastian and other saints is very noteworthy. Every room contains many fine works which I do not notice.

Enter the Sala di Saturno. Right of the door, as you enter, is a Pontormo, the Santi Coronati (see Mrs. Jameson).

Over the door, notice the ** Sebastiano del Piombo, the martyrdom of St. Agatha, whose breasts are just being seared by the executioners; a magnificent treatment of the nude, with the splendid colour of this Venetian painter, still visible after he had come under the influence of Michael Angelo's style of drawing and composition. Every detail of this noble work is worthy of close attention, in spite of the intense painfulness of the subject. Its flesh tints are splendid. The St. Agatha is Giorgionesque; but the executioners are entirely in the style of Michael Angelo. This seems to me Sebastiano's masterpiece. It was painted for a cardinal of St. Agatha.

Number 178 is ** Raphael's Madonna del Granduca, of his early Florentine period, the most exquisite picture by this master in Florence, and, perhaps, with the exception of the Sposalizio at Milan, in the whole world. You cannot look too long at it. Simple, pure, and beautiful; reminiscent of Perugino, whose type it embodies, but clearer in colour, daintier, softer. It has even a touch of his earliest Urbino manner.

Numbers ** 61 and * 59, also by Raphael, are portraits of Angiolo and Maddalena Doni, also of his early Florentine period. 61 must rank among his finest portraits. It is full of thought and earnestness. The hands, hair, and expression are admirable; they recall Francia. In 59, the young Umbrian painter, coming fresh to Florence from the school of Perugino, shows distinct evidences of being influenced by Leonardo's Mona Lisa (now in the Louvre), especially in the face and the painting of the soft

RAPHAEL. — MADONNA DEL GRANDUCA.

and luxurious hands. These two portraits, again, you cannot look at too carefully. Do not overlook the Umbrian landscape.

Number * 172, an Andrea del Sarto, is a group of saints, absurdly called the Disputà sulla Trinità. To the right, St. Augustin, holding a crozier, is speaking with rapt eloquence: beside him mild St. Lawrence listens: to the left are St. Francis, then St. Peter Martyr (or Thomas Aquinas?) consulting the Scriptures; in the foreground, kneeling, are St. Sebastian and the Magdalen with her box of ointment; in the background, a Trinity. Admirable both as a bit of colour, and as an example of the way Andrea could give life to these chance assemblages. This is probably a plague picture.

Number * 174 is Raphael's Vision of Ezekiel, — God the Father, enthroned on the mystic beasts of the Evangelists, and adored by the angel of St. Matthew. This work is full of the influence of Michael Angelo.

Number * 171, Raphael's portrait of Cardinal Inghirami, of his Roman period, is a triumph of art over an unpicturesque subject with a bad squint. Raphael has succeeded in giving the intellectual and powerful character of the face, while the statesmanlike hands are rendered in the most masterful manner. The reds are marvellously managed.

Number 165 is the Madonna del Baldacchino, attributed to Raphael, and in part by him: begun in Florence before he went to Rome, and left unfinished. The composition strongly recalls Fra Bartolommeo, under whose influence Raphael was then passing. The Child, however, is extremely Raphaelesque. The Madonna is of his later Florentine manner. The throne is in the style of the Frate. To the left stand St. Peter with the keys, and St. Bruno (or I think rather St. Bernard, reading, as when Our Lady appeared to him). To the right are St. James with his staff, and St. Augustin with the "De Civitate Dei." At the foot of the throne are two dainty little angels, very like Fra Bartolommeo. How much is Raphael's own is uncertain. The flying angels at least were added afterward, the last being copied from Raphael's own fresco in Santa Maria della Pace at Rome. Later still, one Cassana glazed it over, added the top of the canopy, and gave it a false finish. The St. Augustin probably belongs to the finisher.

Number 167 is a Giulio Romano, Apollo and the Muses, dancing; a feeble work, based on Mantegna's group in the Louvre, and spoilt in the stealing.

Number 164 is an Entombment, by *Perugino; one of his finest works. Yet even in this late composition, observe how the two saints near the right — Nicodemus and another to whom he is showing the three nails (now almost faded) — recall the exactly similar gestures in the great Fra Angelico in the Belle Arti, as well as the Giottino in the Uffizi (compare them). The women are beautifully painted. The head-dresses, the poses of the heads, the treatment of the dead nude, the somewhat vague and vapid expressions of the very abstract spectators, are all redolent of Perugino. Good Umbrian landscape background.

Above it, 163, is an Annunciation by Andrea del Sarto. Full of light and charming colour, but very typical of the change which came over later Renaissance conceptions of this subject. The angel is deliciously soft and boyish.

Number 159, a *Fra Bartolommeo, is the Risen Christ, enthroned in the midst of the four Evangelists. Compare this picture with the Madonna del Baldacchino. The Evangelists, alike in figure, gesture, and robes, foreshadow the Raphael cartoons and show whence Raphael derived many of his conceptions. The drapery of the Christ is masterly.

On the right wall, *158, is Raphael's fine portrait of Cardinal Bibbiena, a work full of his developed Roman manner: but considered a copy.

Number 157, by Titian, is a Bacchanal, copy, in the same style as his Bacchus and Ariadne in the National Gallery.

Number 153 is an odious Carlo Dolci of Santa Rosa.

Number 150 is *Van Dyck's excellent portrait of Charles I. and Henrietta Maria. The faces are rendered with all Van Dyck's courtly grace, and the lace is (as always with this painter) a marvel of workmanship. You can see the very stitches that are not there; the illusion is only dispelled by close inspection. Charles's face bears the character of the man — chivalrous and opinionated, false and yet honest.

Number 151, *Raphael's Madonna della Sedia, of his Roman period, is the most popular but not the most beautiful of his Madonnas. In form, this is a Madonna with the infant St. John. Our Lady is represented by a comely and graceful but by no means spiritual and somewhat insipid Roman contadina. The child is a dainty, well-fed human baby, very charming, but not divine. The head-dress and shawl are pretty and prettily painted. Pure maternal love is the key-note. As art, this is a fine work, but it does not appeal to the soul like the Madonna del Granduca opposite it. Go frequently from one to the other if you would understand the difference between the great painter's Florentine and Roman manners. Compare also the face and neck of the Granduca with the Perugino in the same room, and the infant Christ in the Sedia with the baby angels in Fra Bartolommeo's Risen Christ. They throw much light upon Raphael's evolution. The soft tints and evasive drawing of the infant St. John of Florence, on the other hand, show his increase in skill over the definiteness of the Granduca. But, as he gained in knowledge, he lost in purity.

The room contains many other good works to which I do not call attention.

In the Sala di Giove, right of the door, 18, is *Titian's Bella, a beautiful and beautifully painted portrait of a calmly aristocratic Venetian lady with rich waving hair, which should be compared with the Caterina Cornaro in the Uffizi. The dress is charming. This is one of Titian's most pleasing portraits in Florence. The slashed sleeves are rendered with consummate skill. The colouring is delicious.

Above it, 139, is *a charming Holy Family by Rubens, where the Christ and St. John recall in beauty the portrait of his own baby at Munich. This is a splendid bit of colour and drawing in Rubens's best smaller style.

Left of the door, 64, is a **Fra Bartolommeo, a Deposition; a noble and attractive work, with an exquisite Mater Dolorosa, and a fine figure of the Magdalen embracing the feet of Christ. The dead Saviour is admirably studied. The meaningless face of the St. John, however, somewhat mars the effect of the picture.

On the same wall are two interesting Paolo Veroneses, and a fine portrait by Tintoretto.

On the end wall are two excellent Moronis.

Number 125 is *Fra Bartolommeo's St. Mark, in a niche resembling those beneath

FRA BARTOLOMMEO. — DEPOSITION.

the dome of the Cathedral. (Observe in architecture these Renaissance niches.) This is a splendid colossal work, noble in form, and admirable in drapery, but a little too grandiose. It again shows whence Raphael derived many of his figures of Evangelists and Apostles. The picture was painted for the choir of San Marco, the church of the painter's own monastery.

Over the door, * 124, is a beautiful Annunciation by Andrea del Sarto. Note here, as a formal point, that the positions of the Madonna and angel, to right and left, are reversed from familiar usage. Yet observe even in this work the survival of a formal barrier (the prie-dieu) between Gabriel and Our Lady. The shrinking attitude of the Madonna, with her finger in her open book, is most charming, and the colour is of Andrea's finest. In the background, we get a reminiscence of the traditional loggia, as we do also of several other early elements. From the top of the balcony, David beholds Bathsheba bathing (somewhat publicly), a mere excuse for the Renaissance love of the nude. The two additional angels in the background are unusual. Note the dove descending in a glory on the right.

Number 123, a luminous Andrea del Sarto of the glorified Madonna, with saints, not quite so beautiful as the last, is a Vallombrosan picture, and the saints in the foreground form a familiar Vallombrosan group, San Bernardo degli Uberti, St. George (or San Fedele?), San Giovanni Gualberto, and St. Catherine, whose broken wheel is just visible in the foreground. The colouring is not so fine as is usual with Andrea: but the picture has had hard treatment. Lafenestre attributes the upper portion alone to Andrea.

Beyond it are more good Moronis.

Number 118, Andrea del Sarto's portrait of himself and his wife, whose face you will often recognise in other works from his pencil, is a beautiful picture.

Number 176, a hateful Domenichino of St. Mary Magdalen, is lachrymose and affected in the worst style of the Decadence.

Number 113, by Rosso, is the Three Fates, long attributed to Michael Angelo.

Number 110, by * Lorenzo Lotto, is the Three Ages of Man, three splendid portraits, admirable in their feeling and colouring.

Number 109 is a portrait of a lady by Paris

Bordone. He has painted several stages of the same face elsewhere, I think.

The dark wall between the windows has a tolerable Rubens and various works of the Decadence.

The Sala di Marte contains, left of the door, Guercino's St. Sebastian, and Cigoli's Magdalen, chiefly interesting for comparison with earlier conceptions. Over the door, 97, is an Andrea del Sarto, another Annunciation, with St. Michael in attendance, holding his scales; not so pleasing as previous ones. Beyond the door, 92, is a Titian, the Young Man with the Glove; a very noble portrait. Above it is Allori's Sacrifice of Abraham, after Sodoma.

Number 94 is Raphael's Holy Family, known as the Madonna dell' Impannata. This is a Madonna with a young St. John the Baptist who closely resembles an infant Bacchus. St. Anne has beautiful draperies, and a fine strong face, well contrasted in line and colour with the fresh young skin of a girlish saint behind her. But the whole picture fails to please like his earlier works.

Number 91 is a ludicrous St. Peter weeping, by Carlo Dolci. His grief moves laughter.

Number 96, * Allori's Judith with the head of Holofernes, — a proud, fine figure, — is one of the noblest and most successful works of the Decadence. Judith's strong dark face is flushed with passion and with her strange night's work. She looks a woman capable of such a deed — but not such stooping. Her brocade is painted with rare carefulness for its epoch.

Number 90 is a mannered Ecce Homo by Cigoli. Other mannered works of the same period I do not notice.

Above it, 89, is a pleasing Bonifazio (the second) of the Rest in the Flight into Egypt; also attributed to Paris Bordone.

Numbers 88 and 87, by Andrea del Sarto, represent the story of Joseph, and are confused and not very pleasing.

Above, 86, a Rubens, the Effects of War, is an allegorical picture closely resembling his Marie de' Medici series, from the Luxembourg, now in the Louvre.

Number 85, another ** Rubens, is a portrait of himself and his brother, and Lipsius and Grotius, one of his finest portrait pieces. Note the admirable contrast between the faces, expressions, and gestures of the two jurists and philosophers on the one hand, and of the artists and diplomatists on the other. They represent respectively scholars and men of the world, thinkers and actors. Look long at the rich red sensuous lips and wistful faces of the artistic grand signiors, beside the firmer mouths, thoughtful eyes and brows, and scholarly hands of the two philosophers. These are likenesses that interpret the sitters. The bust of Seneca at the back, the Dutch tulips, the landscape, the fur, the curtain, the books, the dog, the table-cover, all are worth notice. Do not hurry away from this picture. It is deep — going right into the nature of the men.

Above it, 84, is a fine Bonifazio (or Palma Vecchio), full of the spirit of the later school of Venice.

On the right wall, 83, is a Tintoretto (or Titian), an excellent portrait of Luigi Cornaro.

Number 81 is an Andrea del Sarto, a Madonna and Child, with St. Elizabeth and the Baptist. This is one of his most exquisite and finely coloured works. His soft melting tints are nowhere better exemplified.

Above it, 80, is a Titian, a fine portrait of the anatomist Vesalius, not well preserved.

Number 82, *Van Dyck's noble and characteristic portrait of Cardinal Bentivoglio, represents a gentleman to the finger ends, restrained, diplomatic.

Number 79 is the best of the replicas of Raphael's portrait of Pope Julius II., though not now considered the original. A fine realisation of the stern and hard old man. Face, beard, hands, red cap, and folds of the white robe, all painted as well as Raphael could paint them. Another portrait that shows a man's spirit.

Number 75, a Guido Carracci, is chiefly interesting as a late example of the subject of the Penitent Magdalen in the Desert lifted to behold the Beatific Vision. How altered!

On the window wall are several late pictures, worth notice, but not calling for explanation.

TITIAN. — MAGDALEN (DETAIL).

CHAPTER IX.

THE PITTI PALACE CONTINUED.

ENTER next the Sala d'Apollo; right of the door, 67, is *Titian's Magdalen. This is intended nominally as a representation of the Penitent in the Desert of Provence. But 'tis a far cry from the nameless Byzantine in the Belle Arti, or even from the haggard Donatello of the Baptistery. Titian simply paints a beautiful nude Venetian woman, with copious golden hair, covering her just enough to salve her modesty, but not to conceal her luscious and beautiful figure. The alabaster pot of ointment by her side serves merely to tell us this is meant for a Magdalen. Obviously, she has not been fasting. Regarded as a work of art, this is a fine picture of a fine model. Face, hair, and arms are exquisitely rendered. It belongs to the same family group in Titian's work as the Flora, the Caterina Cornaro, and the Bella, — vivid realisations of an exuberant type of female beauty. Compare it also with the recumbent Venus in the Uffizi.

Above it, 66, Andrea del Sarto, by himself, is a fine portrait with a wistful expression. Still higher is a good Tintoretto.

Number 63 is a Murillo, a Madonna and Child. I am too much out of sympathy with this picture to venture upon making any comment upon it.

Number 60, ** Rembrandt's Portrait of Himself, is a miracle of light and shade, where the glow on the face and on the corselet, as well as the hair and chain of office, are masterpieces of handicraft.

Number 58, an * Andrea del Sarto, is a fine Deposition, which may be instructively compared with the Fra Bartolommeo.

Number 57, a copy by Giulio Romano of Raphael's Madonna della Lucertola at Madrid, is interesting for comparison with Raphael's other Madonnas in this gallery. This wall also contains two or three other noteworthy pictures.

On the end wall, 55, a Baroccio, — a quaint little picture of a baby prince of Urbino, — is more interesting than are often the works of this insipid painter.

The Pitti Palace.   131

Above it, 54, is a * good portrait by Titian of Pietro Aretino, who does not look as bad as he was in reality; broadly painted with masterful decision. Note here also 52, by Pordenone, a fine example of the later Venetian manner. I pass over the Guercino, etc. Number 49, by Tiberio Tito, is a pretty baby, not without interest.

The right wall has several tolerable late pictures, of which 40, Allori's Hospitality of St. Julian, possesses a certain value. For the legend, see Mrs. Jameson. Beneath it are three fine half-lengths.

Number 44 is a hard but tolerably good portrait of the school of Francia; number 43, * a charming portrait by Franciabigio; number 42, a delicate Magdalen by Perugino, in his later manner, probably an old copy.

Number 40, ** Raphael's portrait of Pope Leo X., with two cardinals, is a work which should be compared with his Cardinal Inghirami and his Julius II. It represents Leo in his character of art-patron. The picture shows a high point of technical skill, but is far less interesting than Raphael's earlier manner. The blending and harmonising of the reds is excellent. The fat epicure of a Pope is examining a manuscript with his celebrated magnifying glass. The cardinals are Giulio de' Medici and Ludovico de' Rossi. Giulio Romano partly executed it.

Number 38, Christ and the disciples at Emmaus, attributed to Palma Vecchio, is a most interesting example of the transitional period in Venetian art, with recollections of Bellini and foreshadowings, or more likely reminiscences, of Titian.

On the window wall are works of the Decadence.

The next room to be entered is the Sala di Venere. Left of the door, 20, * Albert Dürer's Adam with Eve opposite, is another interesting example of the rigid northern nude, which should be compared by photographs with those in the Uffizi. It marks advance, and is worthy of the great master, but is still sadly lacking in grace and ideality. It is perhaps a copy from the original at Madrid.

Over the door, 19, is Spagnoletto's unpleasing Flaying of St. Bartholomew.

Number 140, by Leonardo (or his school), is a portrait, which should be compared with

ALBERT DÜRER. — EVE.

Raphael's Maddalena Doni, as well as with the Mona Lisa at the Louvre. Look closely at the hands. Note also the landscape background.

Number 17, Titian's Madonna and Child, with St. Catherine and the youthful Baptist, is an admirable example of Titian's treatment of these subjects.

Number 76 is a * fine murky Rembrandt of an old man: gloomily glorious; above it, 15, a good Salvator Rosa, for those who like him.

On the end wall are works of the Decadence; also, 14, a landscape by Rubens, haymaking. Number 15, Matteo Rosselli's Triumph of David, is a good theatrical work of the late period. Number 11, Francesco Bassano's St. Catherine rescued by the angel, is full of the late Venetian feeling. Compare it with the Titian in the same room. 9, * another landscape by Rubens, with small figures of Ulysses and Nausicaa.

On the right wall are good pictures by various late artists; above them, a sea piece by Salvator Rosa.

Over the door, 3, is a Tintoretto, Venus and Vulcan, with Cupid. Number 1, Dürer's Eve, one of the finest embodiments of the northern nude, is admirable in its way, but still lacks the ideality of Italian treatment. Compare with the Adam opposite and with others in the Uffizi. Again, perhaps a copy.

On the window wall are several works of the Decadence, among which 23, Rustici's Death of the Magdalen, is funny as representing a late baroque conception of the Penitent in the Desert visited by the angel.

Now return to the Sala dell' Iliade, the first you entered. The door on your right leads to the Stanza dell' Educazione di Giove, which contains chiefly works of the seventeenth century. The most interesting are portraits near the window by Bronzino. Number 270, Guido Reni's too famous Cleopatra, is an affected and mannered picture.

Number 272, *Andrea del Sarto's Young St. John the Baptist, once a fine work, full of later Renaissance spirit, is still admirable in its colouring (though spoilt by restorers), the red robe in the foreground being even now splendid, while the flesh-tints are ruined. Like the work on the same subject by Raphael in the Tribuna, it departs entirely from the earlier ascetic traditions, and represents the patron

ANDREA DEL SARTO. — YOUNG ST. JOHN THE BAPTIST.

saint of Florence in the form of a beautiful semi-nude boy, finely proportioned and delicately nurtured. This is in point of fact a well-nourished noble youth, with nothing about him of the penitent or the ascetic. The camel's-hair robe and the reed cross are mere vague pretences. The hand that holds the bowl is admirably modelled.

Number 258 is a good portrait by Tiberio Tinelli; 262, Henri II. of France, attributed to Clouet, but surely Flemish (?). Number 255 is a tolerable portrait by Van der Helst, not up to his usual level. Above them are good Holy Families, 256 and 254, by Fra Bartolommeo and Palma Vecchio (?). Number 252, by a scholar of Holbein, is a portrait of the Duc de Guise. Number 245, a fine, but rather uninteresting and badly used portrait, is attributed to Raphael, though of doubtful authenticity, and known as La Velata. It represents the same model who reappears in the Dresden Madonna, and in the Magdalen of the St. Cecilia at Bologna, without the radiance or the rapt eyes. Number * 243 is a Velasquez, a good portrait of Philip IV. of Spain. Many other pictures in this room are deserving of notice, but none of them call for that sort of explanation which is the chief object of the present guide.

The small room to the left, the Stanza della Stufa, has unimportant frescoes of the Ages of Gold, Silver, Brass, and Iron, by Pietro da Cortona, and two bronze statues of Cain and Abel, after Dupré. The door to the right leads to the Bathroom, a florid little apartment, cold, cheerless, and sadly overdecorated.

Beyond it lies the Stanza d' Ulisse, with works mostly of the later age, few of which are important. On the entrance wall, right of the door, 300, is an unusually fine portrait of an old man by Salvator Rosa. 303 and 304 are also good pictures of their school.

On the end wall, 305, by Allori, shows the last stage of the Young St. John in the Desert. Number 307 is an Andrea del Sarto, the Madonna and Child, enthroned on clouds, with various saints, in his latest and least pleasing style, and spoilt by the restorer. In the foreground kneels St. John the Baptist, balanced by the Magdalen with her box of ointment. Behind these two stand, on the left, St. Lawrence and St. Job (Paul the Hermit? Hilarion?), and on the right, St. Sebastian and St. Roch. (The combination of plague-saints makes me think the nude saint is Job.) The picture has been sadly ill-used, and much of the colour in the drapery is quite unworthy of Andrea. The Madonna and Child, however, are well finished. Number 311, ascribed to Titian, is more probably by Dosso Dossi; a good portrait of a Duke of Ferrara, — a replica of one at Modena.

On the left wall, 1313, is a Tintoretto, Madonna and Child, marked by his peculiar smoky colouring and contrasted radiance. Number 318, by Lanfranchi, St. Margaret beholding a Vision, is theatrical and mannered. Number 321, a very unpleasing Ecce Homo by Carlo Dolci, foreshadows later cheap ecclesiastical decoration. Still more unpleasing is 325, Madonna and Child. Above, 324, is Van Dyck's (or Rubens's) portrait of the Duke of Buckingham, instinct with the man's vain and ineffective character scarcely concealed by flattery of a patron.

Number 326 is Paris Bordone's fine copy of Titian's portrait of Pope Paul III. at Naples, — a harmony in red, very effectively rendered. The feeble old man with his half-open mouth and his sprawling hands sits alive before us.

Note those hands well. The veins and sinews show through them in a most lifelike manner.

The Stanza di Prometeo contains several excellent works of the earlier period.

On the entrance wall, left of the door, 371, is a * good hard profile portrait, in the Lombard manner, of Beatrice d'Este, attributed to the Umbrian, Piero della Francesca. 376, * Lorenzo Costa, is a good portrait of a Duke of Bentivoglio. Over the door, 338, is a Madonna with St. James and St. Catherine, of the School of Bellini, an excellent example of the style leading up to Titian. 341 is a Pinturicchio, Adoration of the Magi, where faces, figures, head-dresses, and composition are all highly characteristic of this strongly marked and individualised Umbrian painter (best seen in the Library at Siena). 340 is a Madonna and Child, with two ill-marked female saints; of the School of Perugino, probably by the master himself. 343 is a ** Fra Filippo Lippi, beautiful round Madonna and Child, with the pomegranate. The face of Our Lady is that of Lucrezia Buti, whom the painter married. In the background are two other episodes; on the left, the Birth of the Virgin, with St. Anne in bed, and servants bringing in the usual objects; on the right, the Meeting of Joachim and Anna at the Golden Gate. The round-faced boy to the extreme right is highly characteristic of Fra Filippo's manner; so is the infant Christ. This is one of his best panel pictures, the colour brighter and warmer in tone than usual. Number 339 is a good portrait by Tintoretto. Number 342 is an unknown fifteenth century Florentine Madonna and Child, with the infant St. John, accompanied by two angels. 346, a Zucchero, is interesting chiefly as a late and wholly altered Magdalen, nude save for her own hair, lifted from the mouth of the Sainte Baume by angels, to behold the Beatific Vision (incorrectly described in this and in many other cases as the Assumption of the Magdalen). To the right in the foreground may be seen the cave, with crucifix, skull, and other properties. Above it, 345, is an excellent Holy Family by Granacci, in one of his happier moments; higher still, a pleasing portrait by Sustermans of a Medici baby. Over the door, * 347, is a picture of the school of Filippino Lippi, a Virgin adoring the Child, with the infant St. John the Baptist, and attendant angels, many of them with the familiar Medici features. In the background, marble balustrade with lizard and good hard landscape. The picture looks very like a Filippino, and recalls the St. Bernard of the Badia.

On the end wall, 388, is a Filippino Lippi, the Death of Lucretia, the story told in three episodes; not very successful. Number 349 is a Holy Family, after Filippino Lippi. Above it, 348, is an example of the School of Botticelli, Madonna and Child, with infant St. John of Florence, and two attendant angels. One bears a sword, the other a lily; whence they probably represent St. Michael and St. Gabriel. The baby is ill-drawn and lifeless. St. John's arms still betray the ascetic tendency. Beneath, 353, is Botticelli's portrait called La Bella Simonetta, a literal and unflattering picture, hard and dry, and with little of Botticelli's usual spirituality. It is well painted in its archaic way, but most honest spectators will confess it gives them little pleasure. The ascription to Botticelli is more than doubtful, and the face is not that of Giuliano de' Medici's famous mistress. Number 355, Luca Signorelli's Holy Family, with St. Catherine, is well drawn and incisive, but

The Pitti Palace.

deficient in colouring. Number 354, of the School of Lorenzo di Credi, Holy Family, is characteristic in composition, but lacking the delicate touch of the master. Number 357, Botticelli's Madonna giving the Child to the infant St. John to kiss, is a typically Botticellian (experimental) deviation from the ordinary models. The boy Baptist is very charming; the infant Christ overfed and sleepy. Number 365, by Mariotto Albertinelli, is a Holy Family and angel, in his simpler early Florentine manner, with little trace of Fra Bartolommeo's influence. Number 358, Ghirlandajo's Adoration of the Magi, is a partial replica of his great picture in the Uffizi, with different background and many figures omitted. The workmanship is not so fine as that of the original. This wall contains other good Madonnas by Garofalo, Boateri, and a nameless Florentine of the school of Lippi.

On the left wall, 372, is a portrait attributed (most doubtfully) to Andrea del Castagno. Number 369 is an excellent Ecce Homo by Pollaiolo. Over the door, 373, is a fifteenth century Dominican Florentine altar-piece, attributed (not very probably) to Fra Angelico;

centre, Madonna and Child; on the left, St. John the Baptist of Florence and St. Dominic; on the right, St. Peter Martyr with his bleeding head, and St. Thomas Aquinas with his open book and rays; in the *cuspidi*, little Annunciation; and behind, an episode of St. Dominic Preaching, and the martyrdom of St. Peter Martyr. 377, an Ecce Homo, by Fra Bartolommeo, is pleasing as colour, but deficient in sentiment. 379, Pontormo's Adoration of the Magi, is only interesting for its almost Flemish grotesqueness of characterisation. It has a flavour of Teniers.

On the window wall, 384, Pollaiolo's St. Sebastian, a study of the mere anatomical nude, is well drawn but repulsive, harsh, and uninteresting; the model a bad one. As compared with Perugino and Sodoma in the same subject, it shows the temperament of the purely scientific Renaissance artist. Several other works in this room are well worth study, but need no explanation, and can be easily discovered by the reader for himself.

The Stanza del Poccetti, beyond, does not contain anything that calls for notice in this book. A long corridor leads hence, through

Florentine mosaics and miniatures (some of them excellent), to the Stanza della Giustizia, which contains admirable portraits, and a few good works of the late period. Hondekoeter's cocks and hens, however, explain themselves. Scarselino's Birth of a Noble Infant is interesting as recalling earlier types of the Birth of the Virgin. Vasari's St. Jerome similarly shows us the last stage in the treatment of that familiar subject. Guido's St. Elizabeth is rather more pleasing than most of his work. Some of the portraits by Bronzino and Allori are also attractive in their way. The (second) Bonifazio's Finding of Christ in the Temple shows a complete breaking away from earlier tradition. Sir Peter Lely's Cromwell, sent as a present to the Grand Duke Ferdinand II. by the Protector, will interest English visitors. I leave the other works, and the cabinet in the centre, to the taste of the reader.

The Stanza di Flora contains chiefly late works, of which I shall only mention Van Dyck's Repose on the Flight into Egypt. The merit of the rest can be appreciated, as good or bad, at the spectator's own valuation. I will say the same of the last room, the Sala dei

Putti. It is given over to Salvator Rosa and the Carracci.

The Boboli Gardens, behind the Pitti Palace, afford several striking and characteristic views of Florence.

CHAPTER X.

THE BARGELLO.

THE chief magistrate of Florence in very early times was the Podestà. This office was created in 1207, and the judicial functions were entrusted to the officer so named, who (owing to the mutual jealousy of the internal factions) had to be a foreigner, elected for six months, or later for a year, like mayors elsewhere. Even after the Guilds had introduced their commercial oligarchical system, the Podestà still retained his judicial position. In 1255 (earlier than the building of the Palazzo Vecchio) the town began to erect a castle for its magistrate, known at first as the Palazzo del Podestà, but handed over later to the chief of the police under the Medici Grand Dukes, from whom it derives its usual modern name of the Bargello. The existing Government has fitted up the interior as a museum of plastic and minor arts; and it is, therefore, now officially described as the Regio Museo Nazionale. But nobody ever calls it by any other name save that of the Bargello. It is one of the sights which is absolutely imperative.

Take the Via del Proconsolo, from the Piazza del Duomo. On the left as you descend is the Bargello. Stand opposite and examine the façade and tower. The portion that faces you is the original building (restored). The part at the back is a little later. It takes at least two days to see it cursorily.

The entrance hall, a fine specimen of a vaulted secular interior of its age, contains suits of armour, helmets, etc., the designs on many of which are worthy of notice. Most of them belonged to the Medici family. Also firearms, swords, and other weapons, among which notice a splendid cannon, cast in 1638 by Cosimo Cenni, with the Head of Medusa, the Florentine lion (the Marzocco), the Medici balls, and other devices. Last cabinet, helmet and shield of François Ier of France, of Milanese workmanship. Round the walls are a series of escutcheons. The room to the left, beneath the tower, contains a continuation of the same collection.

BARGELLO (PALAZZO DEL PODESTÀ).

The Bargello.

Enter the courtyard, with its central well and fine open loggia, a remarkable specimen of secular architecture of the thirteenth century. Note the round arches and the columns of the pillars. Also the escutcheons of former Podestàs which surround the court, and the effective triumphal arch on the staircase. Nowhere else in Florence do we feel ourselves so entirely transported to the city and age of Dante. The arms of the quarters of the city in the loggia have the names of the wards to which they belong inscribed below them. Note for future guidance: you will see them elsewhere. The best view of the picturesque quadrangle, with the beautiful loggia on the first floor, is obtained from the corner opposite as you enter.

The works of sculpture (some of them second-rate) which surround the court are sufficiently described on their official labels. Notice those by Niccolò di Piero Lamberti and by Piero di Giovanni Tedesco, from Or San Michele, as throwing light on Donatello's beginnings. Also, Giovanni da Bologna's Architecture, on a fine Renaissance base with Medici balls and feathers; and a Penitent Magdalen in the desert, where the sense of form of the sixteenth century has triumphed over the earlier asceticism which dominated the subject. Baccio Bandinelli's Adam and Eve have the feebleness and vapidity which pursue that ambitious but ineffective sculptor's work. Michael Angelo's * Dying Adonis, however, is a fine though confused piece of sculpture, with a noble face, and well conceived hands. Giovanni da Bologna's * Virtue triumphant over Vice shows the French tinge of feeling and the usual merits and failings of its powerful but theatrical artist. Michael Angelo's * Victory, unfinished as usual, is one of the figures intended for the Tomb of Julius II., of which the so-called Fettered Slaves in the Louvre were also portions. Between the two last is a handsome Renaissance doorway, with symbols of St. Mark and the familiar Venetian inscription: "Peace to thee, Mark my Evangelist."

The door opposite the entrance to the court gives access to two small rooms on the ground floor, with fine fragments of sculpture, mostly mediæval in the first, and sufficiently explained by their labels. The first room has, over the door, a noble Gothic canopy, with Christ and saints, originally on the façade of Santa Maria

Novella. Notice to the left the arms of the wool-weavers, the lamb of St. John of Florence. In the centre, 90, is a Bacchus, perhaps by Giovanni dell' Opera. To the right of it, a fine Renaissance wash-hand fountain, above which are good figures by Simone Talenti. 50, 51, 52, a fine Madonna, and Saints Peter and Paul, with their symbols, brought here from the old Porta Romana. Close to them are two marzocchi, or Florentine lions. I do not call attention to most of the works in this room because they are sufficiently described by their labels: but almost all should be noted and examined, particularly those of the School of Andrea Pisano.

The second room, on the left wall, contains a beautiful series of *reliefs, gravely injured, narrating the life and miracles of San Giovanni Gualberto, founder of the Vallombrosans, by Benedetto da Rovezzano. (They come from the tomb of the saint in the monastery of San Salvi, and were recklessly destroyed by imperial soldiers during the siege of 1530.) 93, San Giovanni Gualberto delivers a monk from a demon. 95 shows the miracle of San Pietro Igneo passing through the fire. 101 is San

Giovanni Gualberto on his bier, Faith and Charity at the sides, mourning. 104 represents the translation of his relics from Passignano, with cure of the sick as they pass (an epileptic boy particularly fine). In 107, heretics attack the monks of San Salvi. These exquisite works, Benedetto's best (1506), deserve the closest attention. (See Perkins's "Tuscan Sculptors," and Mrs. Jameson's "Monastic Orders.")

On the end wall is a noble * mantelpiece, also by Benedetto da Rovezzano, classical in style, representing apparently Apollo, Pluto, and Jupiter (?). This is also one of the most exquisite works of Renaissance sculpture. On the left of it is Michael Angelo's unfinished * Bust of Brutus: the inscription explains that he had not the heart to finish it after Florence lost her freedom: but then, he seldom finished anything. On the right is Bandinelli's insipid Cosimo I.

On the right wall, 123, is a beautiful ** Madonna and Child by Michael Angelo, an early work; not a sacred face, but calm, matronly, and beautiful, like a high-born mother. Here, also, are several reliefs by Pierino da Vinci,

The Bargello.

Leonardo's nephew. 124, a Masque of a Satyr, attributed without due cause to Michael Angelo, is ugly and repulsive, though not without cleverness. In 128, * Michael Angelo's Bacchus, the pose of the figure is not entirely worthy of the great sculptor; but the head and some other parts are most masterly. 133 is a beautiful Madonna and Child, with infant St. John the Baptist of Florence, by Andrea Ferrucci. Beside it, 131, is a * beautiful tabernacle, of perfect proportions and workmanship; beneath it, a good reduction of Michael Angelo's Leda. 134, Antonio Rossellino's (?) lovely * tabernacle for the elements, with adoring angels. All the Renaissance decorative work in this room deserves the closest attention, especially the two exquisite * niches, on either side of the doorway, by Benedetto da Rovezzano. Baccio Bandinelli's portrait relief, 136, has rare merit for this vapid sculptor.

Go out into the courtyard, and mount the stairs, noticing as you go the numerous escutcheons and memorial tablets of city officials and others; pass under the triumphal arch: and enter the loggia on the first floor, with its vaulted roof spangled with Florentine lilies.

This gallery (the Verone) contains a collection of bells, many of them with fine reliefs and interesting or amusing inscriptions.

Enter the First Hall, fitted up as a museum of the works of Donatello. Many of the best originals in Florence are here collected: beside them are placed for comparison casts from Donatello's work in other cities, such as the equestrian statue of Gattamelata at Padua, etc. Among the originals, one of the most important and interesting is on the left wall, the Marzocco, or lion holding the Florentine lily, which long stood in front of the Palazzo Vecchio, but is now replaced by a copy.

In the centre of the room, to the left, is *the David, in bronze, a fine but rather early work, when the master had not yet arrived at his final conceptions of plastic beauty. The pose is a little too self-conscious; the young victor places his foot too proudly on the head of Goliath; and the shepherd's hat shades the face ungracefully: but the nude is good, and the work is still most original and charming. Note how this subject of David colours Tuscan sculpture of the Renaissance. Fine relief on Goliath's helmet — representing Victory. To the right

The Bargello.

is an Amorino, also in bronze, with the open mouth and pose of the hands so characteristic of the sculptor.

On the wall opposite the entrance is a beautiful bronze bust of a young man, with exquisite cameo of Victory; near it, a ** charming relief of an open-mouthed young St. John the Baptist: close by, a * coloured bust of Niccolo da Uzzano, powerful, but unpleasantly realistic. Then, the penitent St. John the Baptist in the desert, a work which should be compared with the wooden Magdalen of the same type in the Baptistery. Recollect that here Donatello is not aiming at pure plastic effect, — certainly not at beauty, — but is endeavouring to realise an ascetic ideal in accordance with the needs and aims of sculpture. In both these St. Johns, the parted lips are highly characteristic. Compare with the plaster casts of two others, at the base of the Gattamelata statue; also with the older type by the first right window. On the end wall is the original ** St. George, from Or San Michele, now replaced by a copy. This is a very noble realisation of the soldier saint, the ideal of chivalry, remarkable for its mingled valour and purity.

Observe how brave and bold, and yet how modest. In this work, Donatello first knew himself. Beneath is a relief of St. George and the Dragon, with the exposed princess, a charming figure, looking on in the background. This last little work may well be compared with the Michel Colombe in the Louvre, as representative of Italian as opposed to French feeling. Compare it also with the plaster cast beneath the Deposition.

By the entrance wall is David with the head of Goliath, in marble — a fine early work whose face should be compared with that of the St. George. In the attitude, which is graceful, there is a little too much of conscious jauntiness. Later, Donatello attains to more modest courage. Close by, a bust of Genevra Cavalcanti, in bronze, is a successful rendering of an unattractive personage. All the casts and originals in this room should be carefully compared with originals elsewhere in Florence. Nowhere else in the world does so good an opportunity exist for becoming acquainted with the style and spirit of this prince of early Renaissance sculpture. Compare particularly all the St. Johns, young and old: and note that some of the

DONATELLO. — ST. GEORGE.

former are the boy ascetic in the desert, while others are just the joyous young patron of Florence. These two boyish figures, St. John the Baptist and David, lie at the root of Renaissance sculpture in Tuscany.

The Second Hall, very dark, contains chiefly tapestries.

The Third Hall, once the Audience Chamber of the Podestà, has a collection of bronzes, pictures, and small decorative objects (the Carrand Collection), impossible to enumerate in close detail, though many of them deserve the greatest attention. It was given by a French benefactor, and is quite as largely French as Florentine. On the entrance wall is a fragment of the School of Taddeo Gaddi, with St. Michael the Archangel and St. Catherine; above it, a quaint Judgment of Paris; higher still, an early example of the Florentine group of the Madonna with St. John the Baptist. The opposite side of the door has several interesting pictures, Coronation of the Virgin, Christ and the Magdalen, Decollation of a Saint, and a charming triptych with Madonna and Child and Florentine saints, reminiscent or prophetic of Filippino Lippi. The Noli Me Tangere, St.

Veronica's Towel, and others, are well worth notice.

The first case contains bronzes of the Renaissance and earlier, including, end, a grotesque Old French St. George and the Dragon, with other quaint equestrian figures. On the side toward the window are beautiful Renaissance bronzes: Hercules and Antæus, Plenty, Pomona, a Satyr, mostly by Riccio, a beautiful Amorino, an affected sixteenth century Venetian Fortuna, a fine Mars, Hercules, etc. I do not enumerate these, or the works on the window wall opposite them, among which note a very quaint Marriage of St. Catherine, but all deserve detailed inspection. On the right wall, farther on, are exquisite Flemish panels, an Annunciation, an Adoration of the Magi, a Presentation, etc., etc.; among them, a good Madonna by Hugo Van der Goes. In the next case, centre, are early mosaics, Limoges, and otherwise; a fine crosier, 648; 649, an admirable San Marziale; 650, a reliquary, with the Maries at the Sepulchre; 654, another, with saints and angels; 667, the four Evangelists with their symbols; a good crucifix, Madonnas, etc. I leave these to their labels. At the opposite side is a fine German Flagellation. All need close inspection. The third case contains exquisite ivories, which must be similarly examined by the spectator in detail. On the left side, 175, is a quaint group of Mercury and Polymela, with Venus and Adonis; 164, Triumph of Love; beneath, combs, etc., very curious: identify their subjects. 154 is a quaint Meeting of Joachim and Anna at the Golden Gate, with Stem of Jesse; French art of the fifteenth century. 153 is a characteristic Burgundian St. Catherine, trampling on her persecutor, of a type which will be familiar to visitors to the Louvre. 97 and 98 form a delicious Lombard fourteenth century diptych, with the Nativity, Annunciation, Visitation, Adoration of the Magi, and their visit to Herod. Note this closely. Beside it, 123, is a charming French casket, subjects amply described on labels. 99 is a French diptych, with scenes from the life of Christ, all obvious except the top right hand compartment, which has the common French subject of the Last Judgment, with Resurrection beneath and Christ enthroned above between angels holding the instruments of the Passion, with the Madonna and St. John (or Sainte Geneviève?) kneeling on either side of him; this is exactly like the tympanum of Notre Dame and the Sainte Chapelle. 95 and 96 compose a similar early French diptych, including a Coronation of the Virgin. Notice the regal and affected French type of Madonna. I mention a few only of these beautiful works, but the visitor should inspect and identify each separately. On the opposite side, 60 and 61, are early French chessmen, kings. 26 is an Italo-Byzantine casket, with antique subjects; above it, 93, a quaint French Annunciation. 91 and 92 are French Madonnas. The type will be familiar again to visitors to Cluny and the Louvre. Beneath, 42, is an exquisite early German altar-front of the eleventh century. 24 is a beautiful Byzantine eighth century figure of the Empress Irene. 19, 20, 21 are Roman works of the intermediate period between the classical and the Byzantine or Romanesque art. All these should be closely studied; the Adam in Paradise, naming the beasts, is extremely luminous. Inspect also the little panels beneath them. 35, the Maries at the Sepulchre, is particularly interesting. In some of these works, such as 35, 37, and 38, we get early forms of subjects afterward conventionalised by Christian art. Search in these for the springs of later motives.

The last case contains arms and armour.

The door at the end has an early (fourteenth century) coloured relief of the Madonna and Child, adored by a Podestà, in the lunette — the Authorities of Florence bowing to Religion. It gives access to Hall Four, the ancient Chapel, dedicated to St. Mary Magdalen. The walls are covered with sadly damaged frescoes, now scarcely discernible. The end wall, with window representing St. John the Baptist, has a fresco of Paradise, attributed to Giotto (more likely a pupil), like Andrea Orcagna's fresco of the same scene in the Strozzi chapel at Santa Maria Novella. This is interesting to most people chiefly because of the (over-restored) figure of Dante to the right of the window below. But the work itself has also high artistic value. The right wall has frescoes from the life of St. Mary Magdalen, the dedicatory saint. Only a few figures of the frescoes can now be recognised. But the series once ran thus, and can still be identified on bright days, beginning at the top to the left.

First, the Magdalen at the feast in the house of Levi; second, the raising of Lazarus; third, entirely gone, Magdalen at the Crucifixion; fourth, the Maries at the Sepulchre; fifth, Christ and the Magdalen in the Garden; sixth, the Angel feeding the Magdalen in the Cave in Provence; seventh, St. Maximin bringing her the last sacrament; eighth, the death of the Magdalen. (I can find no trace of the sister subject, St. Mary of Egypt, mentioned in many guide-books: the opposite wall has the miracle of the Merchant of Marseilles, as at Santa Croce.)

To the left of the empty space once occupied by the altar, is St. Jerome in the desert; right of it, Madonna and Child, by a scholar of Ghirlandajo. The case between contains fine articles of church furniture, including a Last Supper, with Christ washing the feet of Peter. The room also contains other interesting objects: Madonna and Child in painted wood by Dello Delli (?); a crucifix with the lamb of St. John the Baptist in the centre at the back; and a few old mosaics.

The small room beyond the chapel has an early fresco of the Madonna and Child, a good

The Bargello.

vaulted roof, and several interesting bits of early needlework, the subjects on which should be carefully noted. On the entrance wall, the angels lifting the Magdalen in the desert.

The next room, the Fifth Hall, to the right, contains on the end wall (avoid it) some ghastly illustrations of the plague, and other works of a similar character, in coloured wax. The centre case has ivories of later dates, some of them excellent in execution, but uninteresting for the most part in design and treatment. The best are two St. Sebastians, probably votive plague-offerings. In the centre is a fine early triptych, with saints (all easily recognised) and scenes from the Passion. A few early works at the farther end of the case also deserve close attention. In the centre case are glass objects, which examine individually. To the right are Limoges enamels; to the left, nautilus shells, mounted as jugs and vases. In the next case are ivory works, Oriental and other, which are merely ingenious and nothing more. The taste of most of them is execrable. In the last case is fine silver work. Observe in all these rooms the fine ceilings, frescoes, and internal decorations. As at Cluny, but even more so, the building itself is here one of the best parts of the museum.

The next room, the Sixth Hall, contains bronzes, reliefs, and statues of the early Renaissance. All these deserve the closest attention. To the right of the door is a St. John the Baptist in the Desert, by Michelozzo, an early example of the comparative abandonment of the merely ascetic ideal. Compare and bear in mind all these various Baptists: their importance is fundamental. Right of the door is also a fine bas-relief by Bertoldo, of a battle between Romans and barbarians, inspired by the antique, and full of classical feeling. The Victories and nude figures to right and left are especially admirable. Above it is a good bust of the Duke of Urbino; beneath, a reliquary of St. Protus and St. Hyacinthus, by Lorenzo Ghiberti; fine flying angels. The case, beyond, contains fine imitation antique and Renaissance statuettes. In the centre of the room, is ** Verrocchio's beautiful bronze David with the head of Goliath, one of its sculptor's masterpieces. The head foreshadows Leonardo; the curls are delicious; the easy assured pose may be compared or contrasted with the Donatello and the

Michael Angelo. The thin veined arms, however, — perhaps of an apprentice model, — are evidently influenced by the ascetic mediæval ideal: compare the figures in Verrocchio's (painted) Baptism of Christ in the Belle Arti. The whole attitude of this David, in spite of its meagre limbs, is striking and graceful. This work should be looked at in contrast with Donatello on the one hand and with Michael Angelo and Benvenuto Cellini on the other.

On the end wall are ** two gilt bronze panels, the sacrifice of Isaac by * Brunelleschi and ** Ghiberti respectively. These were the panels which were sent in by the two artists as specimens of their handiwork in the competition for the Second Gates of the Baptistery in 1402. The superiority of Ghiberti's design in composition and plastic calm is very apparent. At the same time, the elements of conventional treatment common to the two scenes are worth close comparison. The positions of most of the actors and accessories are fairly constant. Observe the quiet strength and repose of Ghiberti, contrasted with the bustle and strain of Brunelleschi. One is like a sculptor's work, the other like an engineer's.

Beneath these is Lorenzo Vecchietta's fine
* recumbent statue for a tomb, in which a successful attempt is made to put greater naturalness into this type of monument. Above is a good Crucifixion by Bertoldo.

On the wall to the right is a Crucifixion, by Donatello, partly gilt. All the attitudes in this admirable scene are worth careful notice. Observe at how much earlier a date sculpture succeeded in emancipating itself from conventional trammels than did painting. No contemporary picture has the freedom and ease of the Roman soldier nailing the feet of the Impenitent Thief nor of the long-haired Magdalen in the foreground to the left, nor of the semi-nude figure with shield beyond it; nor of St. Longinus (distinguished by his halo) with his hand to his mouth, just above the last-mentioned figure. Study closely this admirable relief. It will well repay you.

The Seventh Hall, beyond, contains the work in bronze of the High Renaissance up to the point where it verges toward the Decadence. Among so many noble works as are contained in this room, it is difficult to make a selection: besides, very few of them need explanation.

The Bargello.

Note, however, the Ganymede and the eagle, attributed to Benvenuto Cellini, with its admirable ease of poise, and its perfect equilibrium. (Compare with similar antiques in the Uffizi.) Also the Antoninus Pius, which is a successful fifteenth century imitation of the antique. Look at Daniele da Volterra's * bust of Michael Angelo; and, close beside it, Sansovino's Christ in Glory. In a glass case is Cellini's sketch in bronze for the Perseus of the Loggia dei Lanzi, differing slightly in detail from the model finally adopted. Beside it is an admirably executed but not pleasing bust of Cosimo I., a subject to try the greatest sculptor. Beyond, again, is a * wax model of the Perseus, differing much more markedly from the form at last adopted; further on, ** Cellini's original relief for the base of the Perseus, the Release of Andromeda, now replaced in the Loggia by a cast: a most beautiful piece of consummate metal work. Close by is a fine Venus by Giovanni da Bologna; also on the end wall his Galatea, a successful figure. All the small works on this wall should be carefully noted. In the centre of the room, Giovanni da Bologna's celebrated * Mercury, too often copied, perhaps the lightest work in bronze ever executed. Its poise is wonderful. It seems to soar naturally. But reproductions have vulgarised it. Fine bronze candelabra and other works. I omit many fine specimens of sculpture, such as the copy of the too famous Farnese bull. Do not overlook the handsome wooden ceiling.

The stairs to the upper floor are in Room V., with the late ivories. Go back to it.

The first department at which we arrive, Room I., has a fine timber roof, and is decorated with several original frescoes, those on the end wall, left, being attributed to the ever dubious Giottino. That to the left, a fragment, probably forms part of a Joachim expelled from the Temple (?). To the right is a Meeting of Joachim and Anna at the Golden Gate, — only Joachim and the two servants with the rejected offering remaining. Compare with other frescoes of corresponding scenes, and you will be able to judge of these identifications. In the centre is a Madonna and Child, with Florentine saints, greatly injured.

The entrance wall has beautiful Della Robbia Madonnas, with crowning hands, angels, and other features. Two of these are the favourite

GIOVANNI DA BOLOGNA. — MERCURY.

subject of the Madonna Adoring the Child. The face of the ** central one is inexpressibly beautiful. Beyond the door is a Madonna supporting the dead Christ, by Ghirlandajo, a fine fresco; further on a fresco of Justice, between two suitors, attributed to Rossi; beyond the window a Madonna and draped Child, of the later School of Giotto.

On the end wall are more Della Robbias; above, by Giovanni, Christ and the woman of Samaria; beneath, by Andrea and Luca, Madonna and Child. In the earlier type (Luca and Andrea) the figures are usually white on a blue ground: later works of the same school (Giovanni, etc.), such as the Christ and the Woman of Samaria above, are in polychrome, and less pleasing.

On the left wall, returning, are Christ and the Magdalen in the garden, of the later period; beneath, in the predella, St. Francis receiving the stigmata (compare with pictures), the Resurrection, and the Maries at the Tomb. Beyond the window are more Della Robbias; a charming little Annunciation, good Ascension, a Madonna adoring the Child (with delicious baby St. John of Florence), a Nativity, and a lunette of St. Augustin. After seeing these Della Robbias, look out for similar lunettes and medallions over the doors or arcades of Florentine houses and churches (Ognissanti, Hospital of San Paolo, Innocenti, etc.). Beyond the next window, again, is a Madonna adoring the Child. In this room (with the next) you have the best opportunity afforded you of learning to admire and love the Della Robbias, especially Luca.

Room II., at the far end of this one, contains more Della Robbia ware, of various ages; over the door a florid Annunciation, not so successful, somewhat vulgar in its colouring; right of the door, a Nativity, with shepherds in the background, ox and ass, little St. John of Florence, and adoring angels. Notice the inscriptions. This work exhibits the declining taste of the sixteenth century. The faces of St. John and the Madonna should be compared with the infinitely more beautiful works by Luca and Andrea in the previous room and in this one. Note in each case to which of the family each work is attributed. The best are by Luca, then Andrea, while with Giovanni the type degenerates. At the end wall is a dainty

LUCA DELLA ROBBIA. — MADONNA.

tabernacle, with angels, for holding the elements; above it a charming Madonna; in the centre, a * beautiful lunette with delicious angels adoring the Madonna. Beneath it is a good Andrea, circular Madonna; right and left, charming Lucas. To the left is a debased Madonna in a circle. On the window wall, opposite the door, is a Madonna della Misericordia, crowned as usual, and sheltering votaries under her mantle. (Look out in future for this specialised type of Our Lady.) Between the next windows is a Virgin between two saints (Anne and Giovanni Gualberto), with donors, by Giovanni, better than his wont; above it a Deposition with St. Mary Magdalen holding her box of ointment; to the left, a pretty little group of the infant Christ and the boy Baptist, rather coarsely executed. Between the second and third windows are St. Joseph, with his budded staff, and St. Augustin. In the next group of subjects observe again the boy Baptist of Florence, twice repeated, and the Ascension, with Christ in a mandorla. The Coronation of the Virgin, beyond, has * the Madonna by Luca, with later added angels in the worst style of the family. Between the fifth and sixth windows is a rather theatrical Resurrection; above it, an equally theatrical Christ and the Magdalen. This again indicates the declining taste of the sixteenth century. So do the Madonna between two saints (James, Giovanni Gualberto), and the Miracle of St. Benedict beyond it. On the end wall is an ill-coloured and unpleasing late Nativity; above, St. Ursula, crowned as princess and with her palm of martyrdom. The Christ and the Magdalen over the door is sadly decadent. Returning along the other wall an unpleasing Pietà is passed. Between the first and second windows is a frieze of Christ and the Sacred Blood, and saints in niches, Sebastian, Magdalen, Baptist, and Matthew the Evangelist with book and angel. The combination seems to indicate a votive plague work. Between the second and third windows are more pleasing examples: Madonnas adoring and otherwise; a good St. Catherine; dainty boy Baptist; and a good portrait of a lady. The support of the central Madonna, by Francesco di Simone (with the face of Christ on St. Veronica's towel, and charming cherubs), is worth notice. In the centre are specimens of fine Italian ware of the fifteenth and sixteenth centuries. The subjects and decorations of many of these are well worth notice.

Room III., below the steps, very dark, contains tapestries and glass. On the entrance wall are three beautiful coloured Madonnas; near the window, another. These charming works need no explanation, but should all be noticed for their truth and beauty.

Now traverse again Rooms II. and I., and arrive at Room IV., at the end, containing sculpture, chiefly of the earlier Renaissance.

To the right of the door is an Orcagna (?), Music, on a beautiful twisted column, recalling those in Or San Michele. The figure is one of Orcagna's ideal representations, and very charming.

Over the door is a late Della Robbia; beyond the door are terra-cottas. Observe here, once more, the dominant influence of the youthful St. John the Baptist, who colours so much of Florentine Renaissance ideals. Here is a *beautiful little statuette by Michelozzo of the boy Baptist starting for the desert. Observe the difference between this subject and St. John in the desert. Then there is a *statuette, by an unknown Florentine of the sixteenth century, of the young Baptist as a recluse; the alternative treatment; beyond it, a baby St. John, with his mouth open; another by Rossellino, much injured. On the same wall are two Penitent St. Jeromes (note the lion), companions to the St. Johns and Magdalens; as well as copies in terra-cotta by Niccolò Tribolo of Michael Angelo's Night, Dawn, etc., in the New Sacristy at San Lorenzo. Note likewise a good head of * Piero de' Medici, by Verrocchio, and other portrait works.

By the left wall is a very quaint early Christian sarcophagus (of the fourth century), with a slight Oriental tinge in its sculpture; in the left compartment is Jonah cast out by the sailors; in the right compartment, Jonah returned to land by the whale. The same subject occurs on an ambo at Ravello. Notice the corner faces, with caps recalling the Mithra reliefs. Above is a bust by Rossellino; a curious early Tuscan Crucifixion, with St. John and Madonna; Madonna and angel; Madonna and Child, by Alberto d'Arnoldo; and a quaint early relief of San Frediano of Lucca. Here also is a * good portrait-bust by Benedetto da Majano; higher up, a picture of the school of Andrea Pisano, Madonna and Child, between patron saints of Florence; on the left, Santa Reparata, with her red-cross flag; on the right, St. John the Baptist.

On the window wall is a sepulchral figure of a bishop, flanked on either side by naïve Romanesque reliefs of Christ and St. Benedict, and the Call of Peter and Andrew; above them, the *Apostles, of the school of Andrea Pisano.

On the right wall is a *lifelike bust, by Rossellino, of Francesco Sassetti, full of character; to balance it, a *bust of an unknown fifteenth century Florentine, with thick under lip, instinct with keen penetration; the sculptor unknown. Between them is a **fine relief by Verrocchio, from the tomb of Francesca Pitti Tornabuoni, the only one now remaining of this fine series. The treatment is thoroughly antique. The figures represent: on the right, the death of Francesca in childbirth, with attendants mourning and tearing their hair; to the extreme right, the new-born infant; on the left, the child brought by its nurse to the widowed father. This is one of the earliest examples of such entirely classical and almost pagan treatment, which culminates in the frank paganism of Riccio's fine bronzes in the Louvre. Above is a * charming Virgin and Child, of the School of Verrocchio. Another, with a curious head-dress, by Rossellino. Also three admirable portrait-reliefs, sufficiently described on their labels. That of * Francesca Sforza is full of character.

Room V. contains works in marble of the High Renaissance. On the entrance wall, left of the door, is a fine bust of a Florentine lady. By the left wall is a charming little St. John, starting for the desert, by Rossellino. Note again the marked difference of attitude between a St. John setting out and a St. John in the desert. On the same wall are a * Virgin and Child, by Verrocchio; a half-length portrait-statue of a lady, by the same; a relief of Faith, by Matteo Civitale; above, two apostles of the school of Andrea Pisano, and farther on, a * dainty bust of a child, by an unknown fifteenth century Florentine. Above it is a candelabrum, one of a pair by Benedetto da Majano, decorative work and children in his most charming manner. In the centre of the wall is a round relief of * the Madonna adoring the

VERROCHIO. — VIRGIN AND CHILD.

Child, by Rossellino, with shed, ox, and ass, St. Joseph, shepherds, etc., and a delicious ring of baby cherubs; beyond, a young St. John, by the same, intermediate between the ascetic and later joyous treatment. A * Virgin and Child, with gilt background, by Mino da Fiesole, has near it another, closely resembling it in type, by a scholar of Mino, in a delicate frame of *pietra serena*. A portrait-bust by Desiderio da Settignano, an exquisite little * tabernacle for the elements of the Eucharist, with troops of guardian angels, somewhat marred by unpleasant perspective, and, close by, Mino da Fiesole's little Cupid, for a fountain, are also by this wall.

On the end wall are numerous reliefs of the period verging on the Decadence; a Crucifixion of St. Peter, by Della Robbia, very much injured; and a Justice, by Benedetto da Majano. The other works, including the Liberation of Peter, by Luca della Robbia, explain themselves or are explained by their labels.

By the window wall is a rather coarse early Florentine Coronation of Charlemagne, partly restored in plaster. Beyond it, a Tabernacle by Mino da Fiesole, architecturally very pretty;

and in the centre, Michael Angelo's unfinished David (or Apollo); a * young St. John, by Benedetto da Majano; and a Bacchus, by Jacopo Sansovino, which is really its pagan Renaissance equivalent. (How readily the one passes into the other is well shown by the Leonardo in the Louvre.)

By the entrance wall, again, are * three good portrait-busts and a charming Madonna and Child, by Mino da Fiesole. The bust of * Piero de' Medici (nearest the window), with the swollen look, is admirable and lifelike. His imitation of the antique, in the young Marcus Aurelius, may be compared with the St. John the Baptist and the Bacchus.

I have said little of these works, again, merely because they do not need explanation. What they most require is appreciative study. Observe in this hall the fine wooden ceiling.

Room VI. has a good collection of seals, and some singularly ugly Gobelins tapestry.

CHAPTER XI.

OR SAN MICHELE.

HALF-WAY down the Via Calzaioli, on the right, as you go toward the Signoria, stood at the end of the thirteenth century a market or loggia of somewhat the same type as that still to be seen in the Mercato Nuovo. It was covered with a vaulted roof, supporting a granary (horreum), with a much-revered statue of Our Lady, and another of the Archangel Michael; whence the existing name, Or San Michele, or "Granary of St. Michael." In 1350, the original loggia was altered into a church, preserving much the same shape, and with a strong vaulted roof, raised on powerful piers, so as to support the great grain-loft in two stories above it. This church was in particular the Shrine of the Trades, and, above all, of the Arts and Crafts of Florence. It stood close to the Palazzo Vecchio, or Palace of the Signoria, — that is to say, of the Guilds which had practically usurped the government of the city.

In the great plague of 1348, Florence suffered terribly. Many persons who had lost all their relatives in the pestilence, dying themselves, left their fortunes to a certain miraculous picture of Our Lady (by Ugolino da Siena) in Or San Michele which was greatly venerated. After the plague, again, several survivors also made rich thank-offerings for their preservation to the same Madonna. The sum thus accumulated was so enormous that the Company of Or San Michele commissioned Andrea Orcagna to build with it a costly shrine or tabernacle for the picture, which still remains one of the most splendid works of art to be seen in Florence.

If possible, choose a Thursday for this excursion; it is the day of the flower-market, when the Mercato Nuovo is seen to the greatest picturesque advantage. Turn out of the Via Tornabuoni, along the Via Porta Rossa, as far as the Mercato Nuovo. Observe its architecture, which, though much later in date (1514), will help you to understand that of Or San Michele. Then continue on into the Via Calzaioli, and go to Or San Michele itself, which stands on your

GIOVANNI DA BOLOGNA. — ST. LUKE THE EVANGELIST.

Or San Michele.

left hand, looking less like a church than a square (or rather oblong) three-storied warehouse, — as in the point of fact it was, save for its ground floor. Notice, first, the beautiful architecture of this ground floor, — the church proper, — and then the windows and cornices of the granary above it. Observe the conjunction of round arches with Gothic detail. Walk round it once for the general effect. Then, return to the Via Calzaioli, to examine the niches and sculpture in detail. There are three niches at either end, east and west, and four on each side, north and south. The statues in the niches were each given by one of the guilds of craftsmen or professions. The arms of the various guilds who gave them are in circles above their gifts.

Begin on the east side, to the right. In the first niche stands St. Luke the Evangelist, by Giovanni da Bologna (1602); beneath it, his winged bull. This is the latest of the series, and was given by the Judges and Notaries. The second niche, itself a beautiful work by Donatello, well worthy of notice, contains a Christ and the doubting Thomas, by Verrocchio (1483), a very characteristic example of this great though rather dry sculptor; given by the Merchants. In the third niche stands St. John the Baptist of Florence, by Ghiberti (1414), with a robe covering his camel-hair garment; given by the Cloth Dealers. This is the ascetic saint in the desert. Note also the little figures between the niches, and those on the summits of the mullions in the windows.

On the south side, in the first niche, is St. John the Evangelist, by Baccio da Montelupo, (1515); given by the Silk Weavers. On the niche above, and in the circle, are the arms of the Guild. The second niche once contained a beautiful mediæval Madonna and Child, now removed to the centre of the church. Observe its architecture. Above it stands a charming Madonna and Child, by Luca della Robbia, in a dainty tabernacle. The third niche contains the statue of St. James, by Nanni di Banco; given by the Furriers. The little relief below represents the decapitation of the saint; that above, his assumption. On either side are the arms of the Company, quartering the lamb of St. John the Baptist. In the fourth niche is St. Mark the Evangelist, by Donatello (1413); given by the Joiners. Beneath his feet is his

GHIBERTI AND MICHELOZZO. — ST. MATTHEW.

winged lion. In each case observe the architecture of the niches.

Going to the west side, stand under the archway which connects the church with the Guildhall of the Guild of the Wool-Combers beside it. Over the shop behind you, notice the O. S. M., for Or San Michele, which you will observe abundantly on pictures and sculpture elsewhere. The Guildhall, with its beautiful wooden canopy, has the symbol of the Guild, the lamb and flag of St. John, many times repeated. In the first niche is St. Eligius (St. Eloy), the sainted blacksmith, by Nanni di Banco (a noble figure); given by the Farriers. Notice, in the niche, their symbol, the pincers. Beneath is a relief of St. Eligius in his forge performing a famous miracle: in order to shoe a refractory horse, he cut off its leg and then miraculously restored it. In the circle above, observe the pincers. In the second niche stands St. Stephen, by Donatello, in deacon's robes, holding in his hand the stone of his martyrdom; above his head, the arms of the Guild of Wool-Weavers, which gave it, repeated also higher up in the circle. In the third niche is St. Matthew, by Ghiberti and Michelozzo, the gift of the Money-changers, whose patron he was (as he sat at the receipt of custom); above it, their arms; and, on either side, two charming figures composing an Annunciation, by Niccolò d'Arezzo (1400). Look up from this corner at the view of the building.

On the north side, in the first niche, is St. George, by Donatello, — a copy, — the original is in the Bargello; beneath it, a relief of the saint killing the dragon. In the second niche are the Quattro Santi Coronati, or Four Holy Craftsmen, Roman builders and sculptors of the early Church, martyred because they would not make images of pagan deities. (See Mrs. Jameson.) The figures are by Nanni di Banco. Beneath is a relief of the four saints in their workshop, engaged in sculpture and masonry; in the circle above, arms of the four trades who gave them, — Bricklayers, Carpenters, Smiths, and Masons, — whose implements may be seen in the four smaller circles — pincers, hammer, trowel, and angle. In the third niche, St. Philip, by Nanni di Banco, the gift of the Shoemakers; their arms above it. The fourth niche contains a figure of St. Peter the Apostle, with keys and book, a very youthful work by Donatello, still almost Gothic in character. It forms the starting-point for his later development. Trace him hence upward. (His early works here may be compared for drapery, etc., with those of Piero di Giovanni Tedesco from this very church in the Arcade at the Bargello. With the St. George, he throws off the Gothic style, and begins to feel his wings. Thence, see the Donatello room at the Bargello.) Above this figure, in the circle, are the arms of the Butchers, — a goat rampant, by Della Robbia.

Now, enter the church, by the second door to the right, on the west side. The interior is very peculiar. It is divided by piers in the centre into two aisles or passages, and has no regular nave, choir, or transepts. (This arrangement is probably borrowed from the original loggia.) All the frescoes in this church, attributed to Jacopo da Casentino (Landini), but probably by many assistants, are greatly faded and little discernible. Note, however, to the left as you enter, the namesake St. Michael, trampling on the dragon, with kneeling lady donor. Beneath, a curious fresco with the wild legend of the appearance of the saint on Monte Galgano. (See Mrs. Jameson.)

By far the most important object in this church, however, is the great Gothic Shrine, by Orcagna, which faces you at the end of the right aisle as you enter. This magnificent work occupied Orcagna for ten years, and was finished in 1359. Sit down in front of it for awhile, to take in its splendid architectural arrangement. It is a canopy in marble, inlaid with mosaic, gold, and lapis lazuli: and it is enriched with endless pinnacles, columns, and statuettes, in lavish profusion. The whole is clamped together with metal clamps; and though shaken and rent by earthquake, it stands firm and solid in its Gothic grandeur. Study the general scheme for some time before you proceed to examine the reliefs, which bridge over the gap between Andrea Pisano and Ghiberti. They are all by Orcagna.

Now, begin on the left-hand side to examine in detail the sculpture of the base. The reliefs on the altar represent episodes in the history of the Madonna, with the three theological Graces between them. On the left-hand side, in the centre, stands Faith. In the first panel, the Birth of the Virgin is represented with all the conventional details; in the second panel, the Presentation of the Virgin in the Temple, with the High Priest above, the Madonna (now headless) half-way up the steps, St. Joachim and St. Anna on either side, and the Virgins of the Lord in attendance close by. (Compare with the frescoes by Taddeo Gaddi and Giovanni da Milano at Santa Croce.) The piers at the angles, supporting the roof, have allegorical Virtues, after the Gothic taste of the period. On the front, in the centre, is Hope; in the first panel, the Marriage of the Virgin, where the attitudes of Joseph and Mary, the budded staff, the angry suitor striking, the impatient suitor breaking his staff, and all the details, are conventional. Compare with the frescoes. The arrangement persists as late as the Sposalizio by Perugino (now at Caen); imitated by Raphael (in the Brera at Milan), and by Luini at Saronno. (But it did not begin with Orcagna.) In the second panel is the Annunciation, also with the usual conventional features. Notice O. S. M., to right and left on the piers.

The picture over the altar, to contain which this marvellous work was built, was originally a Madonna and Child, with adoring angels, by Ugolino da Siena: the one which now replaces it is by Bernardo Daddi, somewhat after the fashion of the Cimabue in Santa Maria Novella, though of course with technical work in the style of the School of Giotto. Ugolino's was the miraculous image which collected during the plague the money employed in building this Tabernacle. Lafenestre attributes the present altar-piece to Don Lorenzo Monaco: it is no part of my task to give critical opinions, but I confess I fail to see in it any mark of Don Lorenzo's handicraft.

On the right side, in the centre, is Charity, with her flaming crown, nursing an infant. In the first panel is the Nativity, with announcement to the Shepherds; in the second panel, the Adoration of the Magi, where the figures and positions are again conventional. Do not omit such minor features as the beautiful angels on the frame of Daddi's picture, nor the statuettes on the piers. The minor Virtues in relief below have their names inscribed upon them. At the back, below, in the centre, is a door to hold the relic; in the first panel, the Presentation of Christ in the Temple, where priest, altar, fire, etc., are all conventional; in the second panel, the Angel announcing the death of the

Virgin. (Distinguish this subject from an Annunciation. In it, the angel bears three palms or seven stars.) The back, above, is occupied by a large relief of the Death and Assumption of the Madonna; below, Our Lady on her bier, with Christ receiving her soul, like a new-born baby; the Apostles in attendance, with other saints, to right and left, and adoring angels. Above is the Madonna in a mandorla, with *aged* features (very unusual), raised by angels; to the left, St. Thomas, with his hands raised to catch the Sacra Cintola, once held (I think) by the Madonna, but now broken off, with her thumb. (Perhaps it was in metal.) This is the original of the Nanni di Banco on the north door of the Cathedral, where, however, the two trees to the right are replaced by a tree and a bear. Compare them.

Do not rest satisfied with verifying this brief description alone, but sit long, and observe the other details, such as the candlestick angels at the corners, supported by beautiful inlaid twisted pillars, with lions and lionesses alternately on their bases. Note also in detail the exquisite decorative work of the friezes, piers, and arches; the beautiful scallop-shells; and the character of the inlay. Every portion of this gorgeous work deserves long and close study.

After looking at this magnificent masterpiece of Orcagna, it may be difficult for you to interest yourself in the other works in this singular church. The corresponding place in the left aisle is filled by the altar of St. Anne, erected in gratitude for that saint's aid in the expulsion of Walter de Brienne, Duke of Athens. The usual conventional group of St. Anne holding on her knees the Madonna and Child is by Francesco di San Gallo. The central arch on the left contains a niche with the wonder-working Madonna from the outside of the church, transported hither in 1781, in order to preserve it from further injury by the weather. It is a regal crowned Madonna, almost recalling the French type, and is attributed to Simone Talenti (?). Of the frescoes, comparatively few can now be deciphered. Among the most noticeable are St. Bartholomew, with his knife, on the pier to the left of Orcagna's shrine; beneath him, a predella of the flaying of the saint; under the next pier, a Trinity. The little scene below can be easily recognised. Under the last pier on the right is a St. George, which remotely suggested Donatello's treatment; below it, the Combat with the Dragon. Under the last pier, in the centre, is St. Stephen, with his stone on his head; beneath, his martyrdom. Many of the others may be spelt out on bright mornings.

I advise you to sit for some time in this church, to observe its architecture and decoration, and also to familiarise yourself with the details of Orcagna's great tabernacle.

CHAPTER XII.

SAN MINIATO.

IT is not often at Florence that one reaches down to the very earliest stratum of Christian hagiology, as one so often does at Rome or Ravenna. Santa Reparata and San Zanobi, indeed, are local saints belonging to the period of the early persecutions; but the ancient church of Santa Reparata has given way before the progress of the cult of Our Lady to the Cathedral of Santa Maria del Fiore, while the body of San Zanobi now reposes in a Renaissance shrine, all glorious from the hands of Lorenzo Ghiberti. At San Miniato del Monte, however, we do really come upon a saint of the earliest layer of Christian martyrology, still enshrined in a church of early date and of fine Romanesque architecture. Minias or Miniatus, according to the legend, was a prince of Armenia, who served Rome in the legions of Decius (about 254 A. D.). Accused of Christianity when the emperor was

SAN MINIATO DEL MONTE.

encamped outside the city of Florence, on the hill which now bears his name, Miniatus confessed the truth, and was condemned to be thrown to the beasts in the amphitheatre — who of course declined to harm him. The usual varied attempts to kill him which followed, all failed in the usual way; but at last he was beheaded, a fate which no saint, not even St. Denis, could ever permanently survive. From a very early period, it is probable that a church on this site covered his remains, which still exist here. The present basilica (such is its official title), a beautiful specimen of Tuscan-Romanesque architecture, dates in part from the year 1010. With the group of buildings about it, forming part originally of a Benedictine monastery, it is conspicuous from almost every part of the Lungarno. Choose a bright day on which to visit it. Read beforehand the legend of St. Benedict.

Another saint, however, with whose history it is also necessary to be acquainted in order fully to understand San Miniato, is a much later one, San Giovanni Gualberto, the founder of Vallombrosa (985-1073). Giovanni was a member of a wealthy Florentine family. An assassin murdered his brother Hugo. By the custom of vendetta, which then universally obtained, Giovanni ought to have killed the murderer. As he mounted one Good Friday toward San Miniato, with armed followers, he unexpectedly met the murderer, defenceless, at a turn of the road. The assassin, taken by surprise, fell at his feet and begged for mercy, for love of Christ and Our Lady. Giovanni, moved by pity, forgave him, and went on to San Miniato, where he threw himself trembling before a crucifix. Instantly, the Christ on the cross nodded his head in approval. Deeply stirred by this incident, Giovanni became a Benedictine monk in the monastery of San Miniato: but afterward, finding the discipline too lax for him, he retired to Vallombrosa, where he founded a sterner and more ascetic order. The crucifix which performed the miracle, and many other mementoes of the saint, still remain at San Miniato. (See the beautiful legend in full in Mrs. Jameson.)

Remember, therefore, three things about this church: that it is the church of a Benedictine monastery, and therefore full of pictures of St. Benedict; that it is the church of the early

San Miniato. 193

local Armenian martyr San Miniato, over whose body it is raised; and that it was hallowed by its association with San Giovanni Gualberto.

Walk or drive as far as the Porta San Niccolò. Then take the zigzag path up the hill, as far as the Piazzale Michelangiolo, on the Viale dei Colli. From this point there is a fine view of Florence. In the centre of the Piazzale stands a copy in bronze of Michael Angelo's David (at the Belle Arti), originally intended to replace the marble figure removed from outside the Palazzo Vecchio, but afterward placed in its present site because the dark background, which suited the marble, destroyed the effect of the bronze copy. At its base are similar copies of Day, Night, Dawn, and Dusk from the Tombs of the Medici at San Lorenzo.

The small church, among cypresses, a little farther up, is attached to the Franciscan monastery of San Salvatore al Monte; it was built by Cronaca in the year 1504. Its internal proportions are simple but pleasing. Above the High Altar is a Crucifixion, with St. Francis close to the Cross, and the Madonna and St. John. (The Franciscans always attach special importance to the cross and crucifix.) Over the left door is a Pietà, by Giovanni della Robbia. Notice throughout the Franciscan character of the decorations.

Continue up the hill as far as the fort, erected by Michael Angelo in 1529, and defended by him for eleven months against the imperial troops, who besieged the town to restore the Medici. Pass in by the gate of Michael Angelo's fortress, with the Medici balls now triumphantly displayed on its doorway, and ring the bell at the door in front of you. (The custode expects a few soldi.) Stand on the platform in front of the church, to observe the façade and the Palace to the right of it (about 1294).

The front, which was built about 1013 and restored in 1401, is in the Tuscan-Romanesque style, and not unlike the Baptistery or the early part of Santa Maria Novella. Above are beautiful pilasters and inlaid work, on the gable of the nave, which is connected with the aisles by triangular half-pediments. (Compare with Santa Croce and Santa Maria Novella.) Over the principal window on the front is a too much-restored thirteenth century mosaic, representing Christ enthroned, on a very Byzantine seat,

FAÇADE OF THE BASILICA OF SAN MINIATO DEL MONTE.

with Our Lady to his right and San Miniato to his left, holding in his hand a problematical object which is apparently a crown (but I do not feel sure of it). Do not overlook the eagle on the top, the beautiful cornice, and the heraldic animals in the gable. Observe also the lions supporting the pillars of the upper window, with its exquisite inlaid-work. The campanile, ruinous, is of 1524.

Enter the church, which is in form a simple basilica, with an apse of the tribune, but with its choir raised by steps above the crypt. As it stands, it is the oldest church in Florence, save perhaps the Baptistery. Notice the beautiful side arches of the nave, supported by columns, whose marble is unfortunately artificial. Observe also that the roof is largely supported by three arches across the Nave, borne by clustered pillars, dividing it into three main compartments. Nave, arches, and tribune are almost entirely covered with ornamental marble decoration. Notice also the inlaid floor, with the Signs of the Zodiac, and animals in pairs on either side of a tree, together with the frequent Romanesque device (once Etruscan and Oriental) of two birds pecking toward a centre.

(See Goblet d'Alviella's "Migration of Symbols.")

In the right aisle are ruined frescoes; the first exhibits, in the centre, the Madonna and Child; on the left, St. John the Baptist, St. Mark the Evangelist, and St. Francis; and on the right, St. John the Evangelist, St. James, and St. Anthony Abbot, attributed to Paolo di Stefano. Farther on are groups of saints, indistinctly traceable. Among them I make out St. Nicholas of Bari with his golden balls, and probably Santa Reparata. On the pier, St. Mary Magdalen, clad with her own hair, in her cave in Provence. Next her St. Catherine, San Miniato, St. Julian, and a fourth figure with a Cross and instruments of the Passion, of which I am not certain. All these are perhaps by Spinello Aretino (?).

Before mounting the steps, which lead to the raised choir, observe, in the centre, the beautiful little canopy or chapel, erected for Piero de' Medici after a design by Michelozzo, in order to cover the famous Crucifix, which bowed its head to San Giovanni Gualberto, the founder of the Vallombrosan order, when he pardoned the murderer of his brother. The altar-piece

San Miniato.

is a composite picture (attributed to Spinello Aretino?), with San Miniato, crowned, to the right, and San Giovanni Gualberto, bearing the crucifix, to the left. In the centre are scenes from the Passion, with an Annunciation, Ascension, etc.

Now, mount the steps to the raised choir, noticing as you do so the beautiful wall of the crypt, behind the canopy, as well as the interesting roof of the latter. To your right, at the top of the stairs, are three saints, among whom St. Mary Magdalen and Santa Reparata with her lily are alone clearly recognisable. In front of you is the exquisite * screen of the choir, a most lovely work in inlaid marble with mosaic patterns of Romanesque type. Examine these in detail, and note particularly the quaint device of men and winged monsters on either side of the doorway. All these figures are lovely specimens of Romanesque work. The ** pulpit, raised on pillars, and with its lectern supported by an eagle, standing on a squat human figure, above a lion, is also a work of extraordinary beauty. All its details should be carefully inspected. Look into the handicraft of all this work closely. Then, enter the choir.

The apse of the tribune has an * early mosaic twelfth century(?), very much restored (in 1388, 1481, and our own time), but still extremely beautiful, of Christ blessing, with the Alpha and Omega on either side of him. Notice the Byzantine style of the throne. To his right stands the Madonna, to his left " Sanctus Miniatus, Rex Erminie," holding his crown, as if offering it to the Saviour. Beneath are the beasts of the Four Evangelists, with their names marked beside them. The detail of this interesting early work includes curious trees, with birds and other animals. The Byzantine type of the decorative adjuncts is well worth attention. On the under surface of the arch by the side are minor figures, alternately whole length in mandorlas, and busts with haloes, divided by birds pecking. In one corner of the main mosaic is the figure of the donor. Observe also the inlaid decoration of the apse, below, with its windows blocked by translucent slabs of marble.

On the right wall of the choir are pictures of local interest; between the doors, a panel of San Miniato, with his sword, and on either hand, in smaller pictures, the various ineffectual

San Miniato.

attempts to murder him; farther on, saints, too much defaced for safe identification. Over the right altar is San Giovanni Gualberto, holding his crucifix. The left altar has a late picture of San Miniato, with other saints, to whom Our Lady is appearing. On the wall beyond is a Pietà. By the steps, in the left aisle, as you descend, is a fresco of St. Jerome.

Now, enter the depressed crypt, the arrangement of which will help you to understand such later churches as St. Denis, near Paris, where transepts are added to this simpler basilica. The choir is supported by small columns, mostly very ancient, with various capitals, all of which deserve notice. The much larger columns which support the roof of the nave pass through the vaulting of the choir without bearing any of its weight. The chapel at the end, with graceful fluted columns, and frescoed vaulting, contains a High Altar, under which still repose the remains of San Miniato, for whose sake the church was erected.

Half-way down the left aisle is the Chapel of St. James, built in 1461 by Rossellino, to contain the * Tomb of Cardinal James of Portugal, which forms its principal object. All the sculpture is by Rossellino. The Cardinal lies on a bier, supported by charming children. Above, kneel two angels, one of whom holds a crown; higher still, the Madonna and Child, in a frame supported by flying angels. The decorative work of the base and sides is very beautiful. So is that of the entrance arch, and the niches by the windows. Observe the mosaic floor. On the ceiling are four winged cardinal virtues by Della Robbia. On the left wall, above the marble seat, is an Annunciation, formerly attributed to Pollaiolo, but referred by Morelli to Baldovinetti. The frescoes, attributed to the Pollaioli, but similarly assigned by Morelli to Baldovinetti, represent the Four Evangelists, accompanied by the Four Doctors of the Church, in the usual combination.

Farther on, in the left aisle, is a Crucifixion with various saints, amongst whom St. Benedict is conspicuous, close to the foot of the cross. Among the others are probably the Madonna and St. John, St. Stephen and Santa Reparata, St. Francis and St. Anthony Abbot. Farther still, Madonna and Child, in a mandorla of cherubs, with St. Jerome and St. John the Baptist on the right; on the left, St. Benedict and St.

Lawrence. I am not quite sure of all these identifications.

Note the fine wooden roof of the nave, and the frequent repetition throughout of the Florentine eagle of St. John.

Get the sacristan to open for you the door of the *Sacristy, on the right side of the choir. It contains *frescoes by Spinello Aretino, extremely appropriate to a Benedictine Abbey: on the roof, the four Evangelists with their emblems (by another hand, I think); and, beneath, an admirable series of the Miracles of St. Benedict. These run chronologically in a curious spiral order, the top first, then the bottom, running on one plane: but for convenience of description, I treat them by walls. On the wall facing you as you enter: above, to the left, St. Benedict leaves his father's house on horseback; on the right, St. Benedict performs the miracle of the broken dish. Below, to the left, Totila, King of the Goths, comes to visit St. Benedict at the monastery of Monte Cassino and the saint prophesies; on the right is the death of St. Benedict, whom one of his monks sees ascending to heaven, along a broad way covered with brocade. On the wall to the right: above, to the left, St. Benedict puts on the monastic dress, and receives investiture in his cave from the monk Romano; on the right, St. Benedict receives a message from a priest inspired by God. Below, to the left, St. Benedict resuscitates a young monk, killed by the fall of a wall at Monte Cassino (note the devils); on the right, St. Benedict observes a young monk who leaves the church at prayer-time tempted by a devil; he scourges the monk, and exorcises the devil. On the entrance wall: above, to the left, St. Benedict mortifies the flesh by lying among thorns; to the right, St. Benedict is proclaimed prior of the monastery. Below, on the left, St. Benedict discovers water for the convent, and makes a lost axe swim on the surface; on the right, St. Benedict sends forth St. Maurus to rescue St. Placidus, who has fallen into a river. On the window wall: above, to the left, St. Benedict abandons the convent, to the joy of the monks, who found his discipline too severe; to the right, * St. Benedict receives Maurus and Placidus as novices from the hands of their parents. Below, on the left, St. Benedict exorcises devils who prevented the removal of a stone; on the right,

San Miniato.

St. Benedict recognises the armour-bearer whom Totila had sent to him, disguised as the king. Now that you know the subjects, follow them out in the proper order. These fine frescoes, with their dignified treatment of St. Benedict and their varied action, are the best specimens now remaining of Spinello's workmanship. They were restored in 1840.

If you return to Florence by the steep steps which run through a cypress avenue direct to the Porta San Miniato, you will pass on your way (according to Hare) a little shrine which marks the place where San Giovanni Gualberto forgave his brother's murderer. But I will honestly confess that, though I have searched for it more than once, I have failed to find it.

CHAPTER XIII.

THE ETRUSCAN MUSEUM.

EVERY great thing that has ever been done in Italy, late or early, has been done by Etruscans. Rome herself was a half-Tuscan outpost, divided between Latin and Etruscan blood. Her arts and ceremonies, nay, some even of her kings, were supplied to her by Etruria. In later days, her empire was organised by the Etruscan Mæcenas and the Etruscan Sejanus. From the earliest date, the Etruscans alone among Italian races showed themselves capable of fruitfully assimilating Assyrian, Egyptian, and Hellenic culture. When the Roman Empire began to break up, Florence became the chief inheritor of Etruscan greatness; art awoke there, as it also did in equally Etruscan Pisa, Siena, and Perugia. Nowhere in Italy outside the wider Etruscan area were great things done; all the famous poets, painters, sculptors, architects, philosophers, scholars, and men of science were of Tuscan blood, or came from regions that had once been Etruscan. For besides Tuscany proper, with its outliers in Rome (I am speaking ethnically) and Capua, Bologna was Etruscan, as all Lombardy, with Mantua and Ravenna, had been of old: while Venice itself was founded by refugees from Etruscan or half-Etruscan and half-Illyrian cities. It behooves you, therefore, while you are here in the capital of modern Etruria, to learn something of the arts and history of the ancient Tuscans. The best book on the subject is the last edition of Dennis's "Cities and Cemeteries of Etruria." But in order to gain a foretaste of what early Etruria was like, I advise you to begin with a brief visit to the Etruscan Museum of Florence, in the Via della Colonna.

I will give but the briefest generalised account, leaving you to pursue the subject further at your leisure if you find it attracts you.

The first room to the left on the ground floor contains very early hut-shaped sepulchral urns, from the necropolis of Vetulonia. The earliest tombs in Europe were underground houses (or chambered barrows) in which the dead were buried with their arms and goods, to lead their subterraneous life as above ground. After burning came in, these smaller hut-shaped urns for the ashes were substituted for real huts, the soul being supposed to inhabit them as the body had inhabited the underground palaces. The cases also contain pottery of early native execution, weapons, etc., which were placed in the tomb for the use of the spirit. The articles so buried included objects of personal adornment, bracelets, necklets, and decorative household ornaments.

The second room contains bronzes and jewelry, mostly of somewhat later date, also from the necropolis of Vetulonia. The doorways are copied from those in the tombs. Observe throughout how the solid and massive but somewhat gloomy Tuscan type of architecture is derived from ancient Etruria, and has persisted with little change of spirit to the present day. This room also contains beautiful black pottery, as yet betraying little or no Oriental or Greek influence. In the glass case nearest the window, objects found in the tomb of a *lucumo* or prince at Vetulonia. The designs on all the metalwork in this room deserve close attention. In the centre case, notice the exquisite gold jewelry, in miniature filagree-work.

The third room contains objects from Vetulonia and Populonia, including stiff archaic stone mortuary figures, of about the seventh century. These exhibit Egyptian affinities. Notice among them the early occurrence of the common Oriental and afterward Tuscan design of the two birds facing one another, seen at San Miniato and elsewhere. The case near the window contains fine black pottery, with native designs; also exquisite gold jewelry. A good case of coins from Populonia, a fine amphora, etc., are also to be seen here. Many of the lamps and other terra-cotta objects in the end case are highly characteristic.

Mount the staircase to the first floor. To the right lies the Egyptian Museum, interesting mainly to Egyptologists. As it is inferior to those of the great European capitals, especially London and Paris, I will not enumerate its objects. To the right lies the Etruscan Museum, one of the finest in the world, and of strictly local importance. Approach it by passing through the Egyptian rooms, so as to take the various halls in the most instructive order.

Hall VIII. begins the exhibit of Etruscan objects, and contains splendid specimens of black Etruscan pottery, of early date, with a few red specimens. It is not necessary to enumerate these, but particular attention should be paid to the beautiful group in and on case B, between the windows, with decorative figures bearing special relation to the Cult of the Dead. Note the symbolic bird, which sits on the top of most of these pieces. Some of the cases contain good collections of domestic implements, placed with the bodies or ashes of the dead for the use of the spirit. All come from sepulchral monuments.

Hall IX. contains early coloured works: those in case I., mainly of native manufacture and design; in case II., made in Etruria, in imitation of Oriental models; in case III., imported from Corinth. The figures and designs on all of these deserve close attention. In the centre are chased silver and bronze dishes.

Hall X. contains cases of bronze weapons and decorative objects, many of them of high artistic value. Notice, in case I,. two winged Genii with the body of a wounded warrior, closely resembling on the one hand certain Egyptian pictures, and on the other hand suggesting the origin of the mediæval Pietà. The same case contains exquisite candelabra and other fine metal-work. In the centre are magnificent fragments from Chianiano; in cases V. to VII. are weapons, mace, etc. In case VIII., notice exquisite jars and mirror-frames from Telamone.

Hall XI. contains the best bronzes of the collection. In the centre is a great bronze * Chimæra of the fifth century, from Arezzo, considered by some experts to be of Greek workmanship. To the right of the door is a noble statue of ** Minerva, lower portion restored, also from Arezzo; and to balance it a fine statue of an ** Orator, admitted to be of native handicraft, and found near the Trasimene lake. Along the wall beside him are bronze figures, some of them of stiff archaic workmanship, representing Tuscan chieftains and their wives, while others, later, exhibit the gradual increase of Greek influence. On the same wall, above case v. are animal figures, similarly progressing from archaic stiffness to the comparative freedom shown in the small bronze of a he-goat. In the case below are beautiful Etruscan mirrors, the most charming of which is one in silver with the Etruscan deities Aplu, Turms, and Tinia; beside it, dice and other works in ivory. The small cases contain bronzes of various dates, similarly varying from the most marked archaic stiffness to perfect Greek freedom. Among the most beautiful is No. 1, head of a young man, of native workmanship, belonging to the Roman period. Nos. 9, 10, 11, and 13 are also most interesting. The labels give the origin and age of the various figures. On the wall are smaller bronzes, many of them of great beauty. Case 1, which is arranged in approximately chronological order, admirably exhibits the gradual change from stiff early figures, with arms closely affixed to the sides, through those where the arms and legs are partially separated, to later forms in which unsymmetrical arrangement, variety of movement, and at last grace and freedom are more and more conspicuous.

Retraverse Halls XI., X., and IX.

Hall XII., a long corridor, contains painted vases, of Greek origin, imported into Etruria to be buried with the dead. The study of these can only be attempted by the aid of specialist works, such as Miss Jane Harrison's "Greek Vases." The earlier specimens have mostly black figures on a red ground; the later have the figures in red on black. The labels sufficiently indicate their dates and origin for the casual visitor. In the central case is the famous François vase, so called from its first possessor, one of the finest specimens of Greek fictile art. The subjects on its decorations are explained on the label. Near it, in the case to the right, are exquisite tazzas of fine Attic workmanship. Beyond them, we come upon vases with more pictorial and less decorative treatment, showing red figures on a black ground.

Hall XIII. contains black Etruscan pottery, in imitation of metal-work, of the third and second centuries B. C. In the opposite case are decorative terra-cotta works, many of them originally gilt or silvered.

The first room on the left contains the smaller Greek and Roman bronzes, removed from the Uffizi. Only close personal study of these will be of any value. The second room contains the larger bronzes, busts, etc.

Return through Hall XIII. and the Long Corridor into Hall XVIII., which contains objects in glass and in the precious metals, including chaplets, necklaces, etc. In the cases are collections of heavy old Roman and Latin copper money.

The next door to the left gives access to Hall XXI., containing life-sized sarcophagi for burial, and smaller sarcophagi for containing ashes after cremation. In most of these the deceased reclines, half raised, on the lid of the sarcophagus, many of the portraits exhibiting well the able and vigorous Etruscan features. The dead are represented on their tombs as if at a banquet, and often hold in their hands dishes or drinking-vessels. Round the wall are decorations imitated from tombs. In the centre, under curtains (which draw), is a * fine coloured terra-cotta tomb of Larthia Seiantia, from the cemetery of Clusium, now Chiusi. In this example the dress, jewelry, cushions, and other accessories are highly characteristic. The figure represents an Etruscan lady, in her habit as she lived, in the second century B. C. For the subjects on the sarcophagi, the reader must be referred to Dennis's "Cities and Cemeteries of Etruria."

Hall XXII. contains sepulchral monuments of the latest and most civilised period, with subjects taken from Greek mythology sculptured on the sides. These are in most cases indicated on the labels. (Compare those in the Uffizi.) Among the finest are No. 7, the Calydonian Boar; 11, the Death of Oemomaus; 17, etc. Beneath these are fine tombs with figures holding tazzas and bearing traces of colour. Near the middle of the room, * beautiful alabaster monument from Corneto, with Combat of Greeks and Gauls, exquisitely rendered. All the tombs in this room deserve close inspection. In the centre, under curtains, * splendid sarcophagus, with painted figures of a Combat of Greeks and Amazons. This is one of the finest remaining specimens of ancient painting, but is said by Dennis to be the work of a Greek artist. It comes, however, from Corneto, and is of local alabaster: the colours in parts are most fresh and vivid. Notice, near the window, several urns in which the deceased are represented as sleeping, not feasting, — this alternative conception belonging as a rule to a later date and almost leading up to the Christian idea. On the wall to the right are several duplicate representations of the same scenes, which deserve close comparison. The most frequent subject is Polynices and Eteocles.

If this rapid survey of the Etruscan Museum

has interested you in the history and art of the ancestral Florentines and Tuscans, pursue the subject further by reading Dennis's "Cities and Cemeteries of Etruria." A personal visit to one or two of the Etruscan tombs will, however, teach you more than much reading. The most accessible of these is the Tomb of the Volumnii, between Perugia and Assisi. It can be easily visited in the course of a drive from one of these towns to the other. The town walls and other remains of Volterra (Volaterræ) and Populonia are in some ways more important but less easy of access. From Rome the extremely interesting cemetery of Corneto (the ancient Tarquinii) can be easily visited. It contains a number of highly instructive painted grottoes. Good Etruscan collections exist at Cortona, Perugia, and above all in the Vatican.

CHAPTER XIV.

THE RESIDUUM.

AND what a residuum! I have mentioned above what seem to me on the whole the most important objects in Florence for a visitor whose time is limited to see; but I do not by any means intend to imply that the list is exhaustive. On the contrary, I have not yet alluded to two groups of objects of the highest interest, which ought, on purely æsthetic grounds, to rank in the first order among the sights of Florence — the Medici Tombs, by Michael Angelo, in the New Sacristy at San Lorenzo; and the famous Frescoes of the Brancacci Chapel, by Masolino, Masaccio, and Filippino Lippi. For I believe it is best for the tourist to delay visiting them till he has assimilated the objects already described; and I hasten now to fill up the deficiency.

A visit should be undertaken to San Lorenzo and the Medici Tombs together. Go first to the church, and afterward to the Sacristy.

Set out by the Cathedral and the Via Cavour. Turn to the left, by the Medici (Riccardi) Palace, down the Via Gori. Diagonally opposite it, in the little Piazza, is the church of San Lorenzo, the façade unfinished. Recollect that this is the Medici church, close to the Medici palace, and that it is dedicated to the Medici saint, Lorenzo or Lawrence, patron of the Magnificent. In origin, this is one of the oldest churches in Florence (founded 390, consecrated by St. Ambrose 393); but it was burned down in 1423, and reërected by Lorenzo the elder after designs by Brunelleschi. In form, it is a basilica with flat-covered nave and vaulted aisles, ended by a transept. Note the architrave over the columns, supporting the arches. The inner façade is by Michael Angelo.

Walk straight up the nave to the two pulpits, to right and left, by Donatello and his pupils. The right pulpit has reliefs representing Christ in Hades, Resurrection, Ascension; at the back, St. Luke between the Buffeting and the Martyrdom of St. Lawrence. The left pulpit

DONATELLO. — BUST OF ST. LAWRENCE.

has a Crucifixion and Deposition; at the back, St. John, between the Scourging and the Agony in the Garden; at the ends, an Entombment, Christ before Pilate, Christ before Caiaphas. In the right transept is an altar with a fine *marble tabernacle by Desiderio da Settignano. Near the steps of the choir is the plain tomb of Cosimo Pater Patriæ.

In the left transept a door leads to the old Sacristy, by Brunelleschi: note its fine architecture and proportions. Everything in it refers either to St. Lawrence or to the Medici family. Above the left door are statues of St. Stephen and St. Lawrence (buried in the same grave), with their symbols, by Donatello. Above the right door stand statues of the Medici Patrons, Cosimo and Damian, with their symbols, also by Donatello. On the left wall is a beautiful terra-cotta bust of St. Lawrence by the same; above it, coloured relief of Cosimo Pater Patriæ. On the ceiling, in the arches, are the Four Evangelists with their Beasts; on the spandrels, scenes from the Life of John the Baptist, Patron of Florence, all in stucco, by Donatello; round the room, a pretty frieze of cherubs. Among the interesting pictures, notice, on the entrance wall, St. Lawrence enthroned between his brother deacons, St. Stephen (with the stones) and St. Vincent (with the fetters), an inferior work of the School of Perugino. Several others refer to the same saints. On the bronze doors (by Donatello) are saints in pairs, too numerous to specify, but now easily identifiable; on the left door, top, observe St. Stephen and St. Lawrence. In the little room to which this door gives access is a fountain by Verrocchio, with the Medici balls; also, a modern relief of the Martyrdom of St. Lawrence. In the centre of the Sacristy itself, as you return, hidden by a table, is the marble monument of Giovanni de' Medici and his wife, the parents of Cosimo Pater Patriæ, by Donatello. To the left of the entrance is the monument of Piero de' Medici, son of Cosimo and father of Lorenzo, with his brother Giovanni, by Verrocchio.

Return to the church. On your right, in the left transept, as you emerge, is an * Annunciation by Filippo Lippi, with characteristic angels. In the left aisle is a large and ugly fresco of the Martyrdom of St. Lawrence, by Bronzino, who uses it mainly as an excuse for some more of his very unpleasant nudes, wholly unsuited to a sacred building. Near it is a * singing-loft by Donatello and his pupils, recalling the architectural portion of his singing-loft in the Opera del Duomo. The church contains many other interesting pictures; among them, a Rosso, Marriage of the Virgin (second chapel on the right), and a modern altar-piece with St. Lawrence, marked by the gridiron embroidered on his vestments.

The cloisters and the adjoining library are also worth notice.

But the main object of artistic interest at San Lorenzo is, of course, the New Sacristy, with the famous Tombs of the Medici, by Michael Angelo.

To reach them, quit the church, and turn to the left into the little Piazza Madonna. (The Sacristy has been secularised, and is a national monument.) An inscription over the door tells you where to enter.

The steps to the Sacristy are to the left, unnoticeable. Mount them to the Cappella dei Principi, well proportioned, but vulgarly decorated in the usual gaudy taste of reigning families for mere preciousness of material. It was designed by Giovanni de' Medici, and built in 1604. Granite sarcophagi contain the bodies of the grand-ducal family. The mosaics of the wall are costly and ugly.

A door to the left leads along a passage to the New Sacristy, containing the ** Medici Tombs, probably the finest work of Michael Angelo, who also designed the building. To the right is the monument of Giuliano de' Medici, Duc de Nemours, representing him as a commander; on the sarcophagus, famous figures of * Day and ** Night, very noble pieces of sculpture. To the left is the monument of Lorenzo de' Medici, Duke of Urbino, represented in profound thought; on the sarcophagus, figures of * Evening and ** Dawn, equally beautiful. There is nothing, however, to explain in these splendid (unfinished) works, which I therefore leave to your own consideration. The other monuments which were to have filled the Sacristy were never executed.

It is generally admitted that close inspection of the frescoes of the Brancacci Chapel in the Carmelite church (Carmine) on the other side of the Arno, is indispensable to a right

MICHAEL ANGELO. — DAWN (DETAIL OF MONUMENT OF LORENZO DE' MEDICI).

comprehension of the origin and development of Renaissance painting. Here first the Giottesque gives way to nascent realism. If possible, read up the admirable account in Layard's Kugler before you go, and after you come back. Also, read in Mrs. Jameson the story of Petronilla, under St. Peter. These brief notes are only meant to be consulted on the spot, in front of the pictures.

Cross the Ponte Santa Trinità to Santa Maria del Carmine — the church of Filippo Lippi's monastery. It was burnt down in 1771, and entirely rebuilt, so that most of it need not detain you. But the Brancacci Chapel in the right transept survived, with its famous frescoes. These were painted about 1423 and following years by Masolino and his pupil Masaccio, and completed in 1484 by Filippino Lippi. The earlier works mark time for the Renaissance. Many of the scenes contain several distinct episodes combined into one picture.

By the right pillar, above, is a Masolino, Adam and Eve in Paradise; first beginnings of the naturalistic nude; somewhat stiff and unidealised, but by no means without dawning grace and beauty. By the left pillar, above, is a

Masaccio, Adam and Eve driven from Eden; far finer treatment of the nude; better modelled and more beautiful. By the left pillar, below, —I have my reasons for this eccentric order, — is a Filippino Lippi, St. Paul visits St. Peter in prison. On the right pillar, below, is a Lippi again, an angel delivers St. Peter from prison.

On the right wall, above, in a picture by Masolino, St. Peter restores Tabitha to life (or, much more probably, the Cure of Petronilla, St. Peter's invalid daughter — a curious and repulsive legend, for which see Mrs. Jameson); and, still in the same picture, on the left, is the Healing of the Cripple at the Beautiful Gate. Masolino can be readily detected by the long and slender proportions of his figures, by his treatment of drapery, and often (even for the merest novice) by his peculiar capes and head-dresses. On the right wall, below, is a Lippi, the Martyrdom of St. Peter, also in two scenes; to the left are St. Peter and St. Paul before the Roman tribunal; to the right is the Crucifixion of St. Peter.

On the left wall, above, is a Masaccio, subject, the Tribute Money, in three successive scenes; in the centre, the tax-gatherer demands

MASACCIO. — HEAD OF CHRIST (DETAIL OF TRIBUTE MONEY).

a Masaccio, the Shadow of Peter (accompanied by John) curing the sick and deformed. On the right side, above, is a fresco by Masaccio of St. Peter Baptising (famous nude, an epoch in art), below, a Masaccio, St. Peter and St. John distributing alms; at their feet, probably, the dead body of Ananias.

Thoroughly to understand these frescoes, you should previously have seen Masolino's work at Castiglione d'Olona (best visited from Varese). But, in any case, if you compare Masolino's part in these paintings with previous Giottesque art, you will recognise the distinct advance in composition and figure-painting which he made on his predecessors; and if you then look at his far greater scholar, Masaccio, especially in the subject of the Tribute Money, you will observe how much progress that original genius made in anatomy, drawing, modelling, conception of the nude, realistic presentment, treatment of drapery, and feeling for landscape. Read all this subject up in Layard's Kugler, the same evening, and then come again next day to revisit and reconsider.

The Sacristy contains a series of frescoes from the life of St. Cecilia, closely coinciding in the tax of Christ, who sends Peter to obtain it; on the left, Peter catches the fish with the "penny" in its mouth; on the right he gives it to the tax-gatherer. Notice the everyday Florentine costume of the latter, as contrasted with the flowing robes of Christ and the Apostles, borrowed from earlier Giottesque precedent (though, of course, with immense improvement in the treatment), and handed on later to Filippino Lippi, Fra Bartolommeo, and Raphael. On the left wall, below, are frescoes partly by Masaccio, partly by Filippino Lippi (Layard and Eastlake), with a double subject; in the centre and to the left, Simon Magus challenges the Apostles to raise a dead youth to life; they accept; Simon tries, and fails; St. Peter and St. Paul succeed; from the Golden Legend: then, to the right, is the Homage paid to Peter, as in the Landini of the Uffizi. The five figures nearly in the centre, and the ten figures about the kneeling naked boy are attributed to Filippino; the rest, to Masaccio. Try to recognise their different hands in them.

On the left side of the altar wall, above, is a Masolino, the Preaching of St. Peter; below, subject with those in the Uffizi, but with a few more scenes added. I think they need no further elucidation. They have been attributed to Agnolo Gaddi or to Spinello Aretino.

In the cloister (approached by a door from the right aisle) you will find a ruined fresco by Masaccio of the Consecration of this Church; and a Madonna and Saints by Giovanni da Milano.

In order fully to understand Andrea del Sarto, and to know what height can be reached by fresco, you must go to the Annunziata.

The Church of the Santissima Annunziata, in the Piazza called after it, was originally founded in 1250, at the period when the cult of the Blessed Virgin was rapidly growing in depth and intensity throughout all Christendom. As it stands, however, it is mainly of the fifteenth to the seventeenth century. Over the central door of the three in the portico is a mosaic by Davide Ghirlandajo, with the appropriate subject of the Annunciation. The church belonged to an adjacent Servite monastery, to which the door on the left gives access.

The central door leads to an atrium, after the early fashion, with a loggia doubtless intended to represent that in which the Annunciation took place, as seen in all early pictures. It is covered with frescoes, whose unsymmetrical modern glazed arrangement sadly obscures their original order. To the left of the main entrance, facing you as you enter, is the Nativity, with the Madonna adoring the Child, by Baldovinetti, 1460. This is ruined, for it was painted on a dry wall, and has crumbled away. On the right is the arrival of the Magi, by Andrea del Sarto, a very fine work, but with less refined colour than is usual with that master. The loggia to the right has frescoes of the History of the Virgin (patroness of the church) by Andrea del Sarto and his pupils. The series begins on the inner angle, next to the Arrival of the Magi. The first is the ** Birth of the Virgin, by Andrea del Sarto, 1514; a noble work, with all the conventional features retained, St. Anne in bed, the basin, etc. The second should be the Presentation in the Temple, but was never painted. The third, the Marriage of the Virgin, by Franciabigio, 1513, is sadly damaged, but has figures recalling the motives in the Fra Angelico. The angry suitor, rejected by Perugino and Raphael, here raises his hand to strike the Joseph, as in earlier treatments. The fourth is the Visitation, by Pontormo, 1516, with the principal figures arranged as in Mariotto Albertinelli, but with no arch in the background, its place being taken by a scallop-shell niche of Renaissance architecture. The fifth, the Assumption of Our Lady, by Rosso Fiorentino, 1517, is inferior in colour and execution to the others.

The series to the left, which also begins near the inner doorway, represents incidents in the life of San Filippo Benizzi, the great saint of the Servites. In the first * San Filippo is converted, divests himself of his worldly goods and clothing, and assumes the habit of the order; compare with similar episodes in the Life of St. Francis. This is by Cosimo Rosselli; less harsh than is his wont, and with a fine treatment of the nude. In the second, by Andrea del Sarto, * San Filippo, going to Viterbo, divides his cloak with a leper, whom he cures; the Servite robes (really black, but treated as blue) lend themselves admirably to the painter's graceful colouring. In the second,

** gamblers who insult San Filippo are struck by lightning; this is by Andrea. In the fourth, * a woman possessed of a devil is exorcised by San Filippo; this also by Andrea. In the fifth, by the same, * a dead child is resuscitated on touching the saint's bier. This is a late instance of the dead and living figure being represented simultaneously in the same picture. In the sixth, children are healed of diseases by kissing his robes or relics; again by Andrea, but less pleasing in colour.

The interior of the church, with its double series of intercommunicating chapels, has been so entirely modernised and covered with gewgaws as to be uninteresting. To the left, as you enter, is the vulgarised Chapel of the Vergine Annunziata, covered with a baldacchino erected in 1448, from a design by Michelozzo, and full of ugly late silver-work. It contains, behind the altar, a miraculous thirteenth century picture of the Madonna. The last chapel but one on the left has a good Assumption of the Madonna in a mandorla, by Perugino: below are the Apostles, looking upward: the one in the centre is probably St. Thomas, but there is no Sacra Cintola. The angels are noteworthy. There is another Perugino, Madonna and Saints, in one of the Choir Chapels.

The door to the left, in the portico, outside the church, gives access to the cloisters of the Servite Monastery, with many tombs of the order and others. In a lunette opposite you as you enter, under glass, is a ** fresco of the Holy Family, by Andrea del Sarto, known as the Madonna del Sacco, and very charming. It represents the Repose on the Flight into Egypt, and takes its name from the sack of hay on which St. Joseph is seated.

At Santa Trinità the exterior is uninteresting. The interior is good and impressive Gothic; about 1250; attributed to Niccolò Pisano. In the left aisle, second chapel, is a copy of Raphael's (Dresden) Madonna di San Sisto. In the third chapel is an Annunciation, probably by Neri di Bicci. In the fourth chapel is an altar-piece, Coronation of the Virgin, Giottesque; the saints are named on their haloes. In the fifth chapel is a lean wooden penitent Magdalen in the desert, by Desiderio da Settignano, completed by Benedetto da Majano. In the right aisle, beginning at the bottom with the first chapel, St. Maximin brings the Eucharist to St. Mary Magdalen in the Sainte Baume or cave. In the third chapel is a Giottesque Madonna and Child, with St. Andrew and St. Catherine on the left; on the right are St. Nicholas and St. Lucy. The fourth chapel, closed by a screen, contains excellent frescoes, much restored, probably by Don Lorenzo Monaco, the usual series of the History of the Virgin. On the left wall, above, is Joachim expelled from the Temple; below, Joachim and Anna at the Golden Gate; on the altar wall, to the left, is the Birth of the Virgin; on the right, her Presentation in the Temple; and an altar-piece, certainly by Don Lorenzo, * Annunciation; on the right wall, below, is the Marriage of the Virgin; above, her Death. Note also the frescoes on the vaulting. This is a good place to study Don Lorenzo; compare these with the two similar earlier series by Taddeo Gaddi and Giovanni da Milano at Santa Croce. In the fifth chapel is a * marble altar by Benedetto da Rovezzano. In the transept, or, rather, the second chapel to the right, the High Altar (at the time of writing, cut off for restoration) known as the Chapel of the Sassetti, are ** frescoes from the life of St. Francis, by Domenico Ghirlandajo, 1485; subjects and grouping nearly the same as those of the Giottos in Santa Croce, with which compare these Renaissance adaptations. Begin at the upper left compartment, and read round. In the first, St. Francis quits his father's house, and renounces his inheritance. In the second, Pope Honorius approves the Rules of the Order. In the third, St. Francis offers to undergo the Ordeal of Fire before the Sultan. The fourth represents St. Francis receiving the Stigmata; Pisa and its Campanile in the background. The fifth is a local Florentine subject; St. Francis restores to life a child of the Spini family, who had fallen from a window. The scene is in front of this very church; in the background, the Palazzo Spini (now Vieusseux's library), and the (old) Ponte Santa Trinità. The sixth shows the death of St. Francis. Compare this fresco in particular with the Giotto, the composition of which it closely follows. As usual, Ghirlandajo introduces numerous portraits of contemporaries; if you wish to identify them, see Lafenestre. Before the altar are the donors, Francesco Sassetti and his wife, also by Ghirlandajo; note that Francis is the donor's name-saint. On the ceiling are Sibyls. (The Adoration of the Shepherds, in the Belle Arti, by Ghirlandajo, was originally the altar-piece of this chapel.) The *tombs of the Sassetti are by Giuliano da Sangallo.

Florence is so inexhaustible that for the other churches I can only give a few brief hints, which the reader who has followed me so far will now, I hope, be in a position to fill in for himself.

Santo Spirito is an Augustinian church, attached to a monastery. It has thirty-eight chapels, almost all with good altar-pieces; the interior is vast and impressive; mainly by Brunelleschi. St. Nicholas is here a locally important saint. (A neighbouring parish is San Niccolò.) The most remarkable pictures among many are, the fifth chapel (beginning from the right aisle), for a *Madonna with St. Nicholas and St. Catherine, by Filippino Lippi; and the twenty-ninth chapel, for a **masterpiece of an unknown artist, the Trinity with St. Catherine and the penitent Magdalen, — a most striking work, remarkable for its ascetic and morbid

FILIPPINO LIPPI. — MADONNA APPEARING TO ST. BERNARD.

The Residuum.

beauty. For the rest, you must be content with Baedeker, or follow Lafenestre. Notice the good cloisters.

The Ognissanti is a Franciscan church, also attached to a monastery. It is dedicated to All Saints; hence the character of the group in the Giovanni della Robbia which fills the lunette over the doorway. Its best pictures are a * St. Augustine by Botticelli, and a * St. Jerome by Domenico Ghirlandajo, — two doctors of the Church, the other two never finished, — on the right and left of the nave. The cloisters have frescoes from the life of St. Francis and Franciscan saints. The Refectory I will notice later.

The Badia, opposite the Bargello, should be visited, by those who have time, for the sake of the glorious Filippino Lippi of the ** Madonna appearing to St. Bernard, one of his earliest works, and perhaps his finest. It has also some beautiful tombs by Mino da Fiesole; St. Leonard with the fetters in one of them will by this time be familiar.

San Felice, San Niccolò, etc., you need only visit when you have thoroughly seen everything else in Florence.

Among minor sights I must lump not a few works of very high value.

A comparative study of the various representations of the Cenacolo (or Last Supper), usually in Refectories of suppressed monasteries, is very interesting. We have already seen those at Santa Croce (Giottesque) and at San Marco (Ghirlandajo). There is a second Ghirlandajo, almost a replica, in the Refectory of the Ognissanti; a notice marks the door, just beyond the church. The Franciscans wanted to have as good a picture as their Dominican brethren. The room contains several other interesting works both in painting and sculpture. A far more lovely Last Supper is that known as the ** Cenacolo di Fuligno, in the Via Faenza; notice on the door. It occupies the end wall of the Refectory of the old monastery of Sant' Onofrio, and belongs to the School of Perugino. It was once attributed to Raphael, and more lately has been assigned to Gerino da Pistoja; if so, it is by many stages his finest work. Whoever painted it, however, it is one of the most beautiful things in Florence. Yet another Last Supper is to be found in the Refectory of the old Convent of Sant' Apollonia in the street of the same name; it is by Andrea del Castagno, a large number of whose other works have lately been transferred hither, so that this little museum offers the best opportunity of studying that able and vigorous but harsh and soulless master. See also the * Andrea del Sarto at San Salvi. I advise a visit to these four little shows in close succession. Read Mrs. Jameson on the subject beforehand, or take her with you.

If possible walk one day through the Hospital of Santa Maria Nuova, founded by Folco Portinari (father of Dante's Beatrice), and full of memories of the Portinari family. Then, visit the little picture gallery of the Hospital. It contains many objects of interest, and two masterpieces. One is a ** triptych by Hugo van der Goes, the Flemish painter, produced for Tommaso Portinari, agent of the Medici at Bruges, and brought by him to Florence; it is doubtless the finest Flemish work in the city. In the centre is the Nativity, with St. Joseph (?) and adoring shepherds, as well as charming angels, and some exquisite irises. Every straw, every columbine, every vase in his admirable work should be minutely noticed.

In the left wing, are the donor's wife and daughter, presented by their patron saints, St. Mary Magdalen, with her alabaster box, and St. Margaret, with her dragon; on the right wing, the donor and his two sons, presented by St. Matthew (?) and St. Anthony Abbot. This work deserves long and attentive study. In the next room is a * Last Judgment, by Fra Bartolommeo and Mariotto Albertinelli, much damaged, but important as a link in a long chain of similar subjects. See in this connection the great fresco in the Campo Santo at Pisa, the one at Santa Maria Novella, by Orcagna, the panel here, to collate with it, and finally Michael Angelo's marvellous modernisation in the Sistine Chapel of the Vatican, which takes many points from this and the earlier representations. The rooms also contain several other interesting pictures.

The Chapter-house of the Convent of Santa Maria Maddalena dei Pazzi (a local saint, belonging to the Pazzi family; see Santa Croce), contains a noble ** Crucifixion by Perugino, one of the finest single pictures in Florence. It is in three compartments. In the centre is a Crucifixion, with Mary Magdalen, kneeling; left and right are the Madonna and St. John, standing; and St. Bernard and St. Benedict kneeling. The remarkable abstractness and isolation of Perugino's figures is nowhere more observable; it comes out even in the three trees of the left background.

The Spedale degli Innocenti, or Foundling Hospital, near the Annunziata, should be visited both for its charming babies, by Andrea della Robbia, and for its beautiful ** altar-piece of the Adoration of the Magi, with St. John the Baptist of Florence presenting two of the massacred Innocents, by Domenico Ghirlandajo. This is a lovely and appropriate picture, the full meaning of which you will now be in a position to understand. (The church is dedicated to the Holy Innocents.) The lovely landscape and accessories need no bush. In the background, the Massacre of the Innocents, the Announcement to the Shepherds, etc. A masterpiece to study.

For everything else within the town, I must hand you over to Baedeker, Hare, Miss Horner, and Lafenestre.

A stray afternoon may well be devoted to the queer little church of San Leonardo in

Arcetri, outside the town, on the south side of the Arno. To reach it, cross the Ponte Vecchio, and take the second turn on your left, under an arch that spans the roadway. Then follow the steep paved way of the Via della Costa San Giorgio (which will probably reveal to you an unexpected side of Florence). The Porta San Giorgio, which pierces the old walls at the top, has a fresco of the Madonna, between St. George and St. Leonard, the latter bearing the fetters which are his usual symbol; on its outer face is a good relief of St. George and the Dragon. (Note relevancy to the parishes of San Giorgio, below, and San Leonardo, above it.) Follow the road straight to the little church of San Leonardo on your left. (If closed, ring at the door of the cottage in the garden to the right of its façade.)

The chief object of interest within is the pulpit, with rude reliefs of the twelfth century, said to be the oldest surviving pulpit carvings, brough thither from San Pietro Scheraggio, near the Palazzo Vecchio. It has been suggested that these quaint old works gave hints to Niccolò Pisano for his famous and beautiful pulpit in the Baptistery at Pisa. But it must also be remembered, first, that these subjects already show every trace of being conventionalised, so that in all probability many such pulpits once existed, of which Niccolò's is only the finest artistic outcome; and, second, that the figure here which most suggests (or rather foreshadows) Niccolò (the recumbent Madonna in the Nativity) is the analogue of the very one in which that extraordinary genius most closely imitated an antique model in the Campo Santo at Pisa. We may, therefore, conclude that Niccolò merely adopted a conventional series, common at this time, of which this is an early and inferior example, but that he marvellously vivified it by quasi-antique treatment of the faces, figures, draperies, and attitudes, at the same time that he immensely enriched the composition after the example of the antique sarcophagi. The series as it at present exists on this pulpit is out of chronological order, doubtless owing to incorrect putting together at the transference hither. The scenes are, from left to right, the Presentation in the Temple; the Baptism of Christ; the Adoration of the Magi; the Madonna rising from the stem of Jesse; the Deposition from the Cross; and the Nativity. All should be closely observed as early embodiments of the scenes they represent.

Among the older pictures in the church, the most interesting are, on the same wall, the Madonna dropping the Sacra Cintola to St. Thomas, attended by St. Peter, St. Jerome, etc.; and, on the opposite wall, Madonna with St. Leonard (holding the fetters) and other saints readily recognised.

You can vary the walk, on your return, by diverging just outside the gate and following the path which leads along the old walls, with delicious glimpses across the ravine toward the Piazzale, and reëntering the town at Porta San Miniato.

I am always grateful to a book, however inadequate, which has taught me something. Nobody could be more aware than its author of the shortcomings of this one. I shall be content if my readers find, among many faults, that it has helped to teach them how to see Florence. Others may know Florence more intimately: no one could love it better.

THE END.

INDEX.

Agnolo Gaddi (see Gaddi, Agnolo).
Albertinelli, Mariotto, Visitation, 50–51, Holy Family, 141, Last Judgment, 236.
Alberto d'Arnoldo, Madonna and Child, 172.
Aldegrever, Madonna and Child, 67.
Alfani, Holy Family, 56–57.
Alfonso Parigi (see Parigi, Alfonso).
Allori, Alessandro, copy of Judith, 55, Infant Christ, 63, Sacrifice of Abraham, 125, Judith, 126, Hospitality of St. Julian, 131, Young St. John in the Desert, 136, portrait, 143.
Ammanati, Bartolommeo, fountain by, 5.
Andrea del Castagno, 87, portrait, 141, Last Supper, 234–235.
Andrea del Sarto, Madonna and Child, 43–44, St. James, 51, Madonna and Child, 55, portraits, 56, Assumption, 111, Assumption, 114, portrait of himself, 114, group of saints, 117, Annunciation, 119, Annunciation, 123, Madonna and Saints, 124, portrait of himself and his wife, 124, Annunciation, 125, Story of Joseph, 126, Madonna and Child, 127, portrait of himself, 130, Deposition, 130, Young St. John the Baptist, 135–136, Madonna and Child, 136–137, 225, Birth of the Virgin, 226, Life of San Filippo Benizzi, 227–228, Madonna del Sacco, 229, Last Supper, 235.
Andrea Pisano (see Pisano, Andrea).
Angelico, Fra, 19, Coronation of the Virgin, 41, Adoration of the Virgin, 52–55, John the Baptist, 54, Death of the Madonna, 54, Madonna and Child, 89–90, altar-piece, 141–142.
Annibale Carracci (see Carracci, Annibale).
Annunziata, Church of the, 225–229.

Index.

Antonio Pollaiolo (see Pollaiolo, Antonio).
Aretino, Pietro, portrait of, 131.
Aretino, Spinello (see Spinello Aretino).
Arezzo, Niccolò d' (see Niccolò d'Arezzo).
Arnoldo, Alberto d' (see Alberto d'Arnoldo).
Arnolfo di Cambio, erection of the Palazzo Vecchio, 2.

Baccio Bandinelli (see Bandinelli, Baccio).
Baccio da Montelupo, statue of St. John the Evangelist, 180.
Badia, 233.
Baldovinetti, Annunciation, 26, Madonna and Child, 26–27, Annunciation, 200, frescoes, 200, Nativity, 226.
Banco, Nanni di, 47, statue of St. James, 180, statue of St. Eloy, 181, Quattro Santi Coronati, 182, St. Philip, 182, 187.
Bandinelli, Baccio, copy of the Laocoon, 105–106, Adam and Eve, 148, Cosimo I., 250, portrait relief, 151.
Baroccio, copy from Madonna and Child by Correggio, 112, portrait of a baby prince of Urbino, 130.
Bargello, 1, 145–176.
Bartolommeo Ammanati (see Ammanati, Bartolommeo).
Bartolommeo, Fra, 9, design for Madonna and Child, 44, 54, Circumcision and Nativity, 56, Job and Isaiah, 58, Enthroned Madonna, 112–113, Risen Christ, 119–120, Deposition, 122, St. Mark, 122–123, Holy Family, 135, Ecce Homo, 142, Last Judgment, 236.
Bassano, Francesco, St. Catherine, 133.
Bassano, Jacopo, portrait group, 71, Moses and the Burning Bush, 72, Christ in the House of Lazarus, 109–110.
Beccadelli, portrait of, 61.
Bellini, Giovanni, Madonna by the Lake, 75–76, 77, 81.
Benci di Cione, completion of the Loggia dei Lanzi, 3.
Benedetto da Majano, portrait-bust, 172–173, candelabrum, 174, Justice, 175, St. John, 176, Magdalen, 229.
Benedetto da Rovezzano, reliefs of the life of San Giovanni Gualberto, 149–150, mantelpiece, 150, niches, 151, marble altar, 230.
Benozzo Gozzoli, predella, 84.
Bentivoglio, Cardinal, portrait of, 128.
Benvenuto Cellini (see Cellini, Benvenuto).
Bernardo Daddi (see Daddi, Bernardo).
Bertoldi, bas-relief, 162, crucifixion, 164.
Bibbiena, Cardinal, portrait of, 120.
Bicci di Lorenzo, St. Cosimo

Index.

and St. Damian, 24, 26, 43.
Bicci, Neri di (see Neri di Bicci).
Biliverti, Angel with Tobias and Tobit, 113.
Boateri, Madonna, 141.
Bologna, Giovanni da (see Giovanni da Bologna).
Bonifazio, Last Supper, 82, portrait, 111, Rest in the Flight into Egypt, 126, 127, Christ in the Temple, 143.
Bordone, Paris, portraits, 70, portrait, 78, portrait, 80, portrait, 124–125, Rest in the Flight into Egypt, 126, copy of Titian's portrait of Paul III., 137–138.
Botticelli, Madonna, 27, Madonna and Child, 37–38, Annunciation, 39–40, Coronation of the Virgin, 40, Madonna Enthroned, 40, Strength, 40–41, Adoration of the Magi, 51, Calumny, 53, Judith with the Head of Holofernes, 54, St. Sebastian, 55, Holofernes, 56, Adoration of the Magi, 88–89, Birth of Venus, 90–91, La Bella Simonetta, 140, Madonna and Child, 141, St. Augustine, 143.
Breton, Jules, portrait of himself, 92.
Brancacci Chapel, 215.
Bronzino, Christ Releasing Souls from Hades, 41–42, 43, portrait, 44, 54, Dead Christ, 55, 92, portrait of Cosimo I., 112, portraits, 134, portrait, 143, Martyrdom of St. Lawrence, 218–219.
Brunelleschi, design of the Pitti Palace, 107, 108, Sacrifice of Isaac, 163, design of the church of San Lorenzo, sacristy of San Lorenzo, 217–218.

Cabanel, portrait of himself, 92.
Cambio, Arnolfo di (see Arnolfo di Cambio).
Carlo Dolci (see Dolci, Carlo).
Caroto, portrait of Gattamelata, 72–73.
Carpaccio, fragment, 17.
Carracci, Annibale, Christ in Glory, 111–112.
Carracci, Guido, the Penitent Magdalen, 128.
Casentino, Jacopo da (see Jacopo da Casentino).
Castagno, Andrea del (see Andrea del Castagno).
Caterina Cornaro (see Cornaro, Caterina).
Cellini, Benvenuto, statue of Perseus, 6–7, 98, 104, Ganymede, 165, sketch in bronze for the Perseus, bust of Cosimo I.,165, wax model of the Perseus, 165, Release of Andromeda, 165.
Cenni, Cosimo, cannon, 146.
Cigoli, St. Francis receiving the Stigmata, 54–55, Magdalen, 125, Ecce Homo, 126.
Cima da Conegliano, Madonna, 76–77, 81.

Index.

Cione, Benci di (see Benci di Cione).
Civitale, Matteo, relief of Faith, 174.
Clouet, portrait of Henri I., 69, Henri II., 135.
Conegliano, Cima da (see Cima da Conegliano).
Cornaro, Caterina, portrait of, 74.
Cornaro, Luigi, portrait of, 127.
Correggio, Repose on the Flight into Egypt, 62–63, 112.
Cortona, Pietro da (see Pietro da Cortona).
Cosimo I., statue of, 5, portrait of, 112, bust of, 165.
Cosimo Pater Patriæ, tomb of, 217.
Cosimo, Piero di (see Piero di Cosimo).
Cosimo Rosselli (see Rosselli, Cosimo).
Costa, Lorenzo, portrait of a Duke of Bentivoglio, 138.
Cranach, Adam and Eve, 62, portraits of Luther and Melancthon, 65, 92.
Credi, Lorenzo di (see Lorenzo di Credi).
Cristoforo, Filippo di (see Filippo di Cristoforo).
Cristus, Petrus (see Petrus Cristus).

Daddi, Bernardo, altar-piece, St. Matthew and St. Nicholas, 17, Madonna, 185–188.
Daniele da Volterra, bust of Michael Angelo, 165.

David, Gerard, Adoration of the Magi, 67.
Della Robbia (see Robbia, Della).
Delli, Dello, Madonna and Child, 160.
Desiderio da Settignano, tabernacle, 175, tabernacle, 217, Magdalen, 229.
Dolci, Carlo, Santa Rosa, 120, St. Peter, 125, Ecce Homo, 137.
Domenichino, St. Mary Magdalen, 124.
Domenico Veneziano (see Veneziano, Domenico).
Donatello, bronze statue of Judith with the Head of Holofernes, 7, 26, 147, Marzocco, 152, David, 152, Amorino, 153, portrait bust cameo, 153, St. John the Baptist, 153, portrait bust of Niccolo da Uzzano, 153, St. John the Baptist, 153, St. George, 153–154, David, 154, bust of Genevra Cavalcanti, 154, Crucifixion, 164, niche, 179, statue of St. Mark, 180–181, St. Stephen, 181, copy of the St. George, 182, St. Peter, 182–183, pulpits, 216–217, monument of Giovanni de' Medici and his wife, 218.
Don Lorenzo Monaco (see Lorenzo Monaco).
Dossi, Dosso, portrait of a Duke of Ferrara, 137.
Dou, Gerard, 64.
Dürer, Adoration of the Magi, 59–60, St. Philip and St.

Index.

James, 65, portrait of his father, 65, Adam and Eve, 132, Eve, 133-134.

Empoli, Jacopo da (see Jacopo da Empoli).
Este, Beatrice d', portrait of, 138.
Etruscan Museum, 204-214.

Fabriano, Gentile da (see Gentile da Fabriano).
Fedi, group of the Rape of Polyxena, 8.
Ferrucci, Andrea, Madonna and Child, 151.
Fiesole, Mino da (see Mino da Fiesole).
Filippo di Cristoforo, statues of Madonna and Child, St. Dominic, and St. Mary Magdalen, 4.
Filippino Lippi (see Lippi, Filippino).
Filippo Lippi (see Lippi, Filippo).
Fiorentino, Rosso, Assumption of the Madonna, 227.
Flaminio Vacca (see Vacca, Flaminio).
Floris, Adam and Eve, 67.
Foundling Hospital (Spedale degli Innocenti), 237.
Fra Angelico (see Angelico, Fra).
Fra Bartolommeo (see Bartolommeo, Fra).
Francesca, Piero della (see Piero della Francesca).
Francesco di Simone, Madonna, 170.
Francesco Talenti, Simone di (see Simone di Francesco Talenti).
Francia, Francesco, portrait, 58.
Francia, Giacomo, portrait, 114.
Franciabigio, Temple of Hercules, 37, Madonna of the Well, 58, portrait, 131, Marriage of the Virgin, 226-227.
Franco, Raffaello di (see Raffaello di Franco).
Froment, Nicolas, triptych, 68.

Gaddi, Agnolo, design of the frieze of the Loggia dei Lanzi, 6, Annunciation, 19-20, frescoes, life of St. Cecilia, 224-225.
Gaddi, Taddeo, 185, 230.
Garofalo, Annunciation, 63, Madonna, 141.
Gattamelata, portrait of, 72-73.
Gentile da Fabriano, figures of saints from an altarpiece, 83-84.
Gerard David (see David, Gerard).
Gerard Dou (see Dou, Gerard).
Gerino da Pistoia, Madonna and Saints, 29-30, Last Supper, 234.
Ghiberti, Lorenzo, reliquary, Sacrifice of Isaac, 163, St. John the Baptist, 180, statue of St. Matthew, 180-181, 184, 190.
Ghirlandajo, Davide, mosaic, Annunciation, 225.

Ghirlandajo, Domenico, Adoration of the Magi, 32–33, Madonna and Child, 89, Adoration of the Magi, 141, Madonna and dead Christ, 167, frescoes, life of St. Francis, 231–232, St. Jerome, 233, Last Supper, 234, Adoration of the Magi, 237.

Ghirlandajo, Ridolfo, Annunciation, 32, Miracles of San Zanobi, 49–50, portrait, 111, portrait, 113.

Giorgione, portrait of Gattamelata, 72–73, Judgment of Solomon, 81–82, Moses, 82, portrait of a Knight of Malta, 82.

Giottino, Deposition from the Cross, 19, 166.

Giotto, Agony in the Garden, 14, fresco of Paradise, 159, 231.

Giovanni Bellini (see Bellini, Giovanni).

Giovanni da Bologna, bronze statue of Cosimo I. by, 5, marble group of the Rape of the Sabines, 8, Hercules slaying Nessus, 8, 95, figure of Architecture, 147, Virtue Triumphant over Vice, 148, Venus, Galatea, 165, Mercury, 165–166, figure of St. Luke, 179.

Giovanni da Milano, altarpiece, 21, 110, Madonna and Saints, 225, 230.

Giovanni dell' Opera, Bacchus, 149.

Giovanni Tedesco, Piero di (see Piero di Giovanni Tedesco).

Giulio Romano (see Romano, Giulio).

Giuliano da Sangallo, tombs of the Sassetti, 232.

Gozzoli, Benozzo (see Benozzo Gozzoli).

Granacci, Madonna and St. Thomas, 47, Madonna and Child, 113, Holy Family, 139.

Guercino, Sibyl, 61, St. Sebastian, 125, 131.

Guido Carracci (see Carracci, Guido).

Guido da Siena, Madonna, 14.

Guido Reni, portrait of himself, 92, Cleopatra, 134, St. Elizabeth, 143.

Heemskerck, 64.
Holbein, portrait of Richard Southwell, 65, 92.

Innocenti, Spedale degli, 237.
Ingres, portrait, 92.

Jacopo Bassano (see Bassano, Jacopo).

Jacopo da Casentino, Glory of St. Peter, 31–32, frescoes, 183.

Jacopo da Empoli, St. Ivo, 45, Sacrifice of Abraham, 54.

Jan Van Eyck (see Van Eyck, Jan).

Joost Van Cleef (see Van Cleef, Joost).

Julius II., portrait of, 128.

Index.

Kaufmann, Angelica, portrait of herself, 92.
Kulmbach, crucifixion of St. Peter, 67.

Landini (see Jacopo di Casentino).
Le Brun, Mme., portrait of herself, 92.
Leighton, portrait of himself, 92.
Lely, Sir Peter, portrait of Cromwell, 143.
Leonardo da Vinci, 9, Annunciation, 32, 35, 39, Adoration of the Magi, 48, Medusa, 55-56, portrait, 56, the Fornarina, 58-59, portrait, 132-133.
Leyden, Lucas van, Crown of Thorns, 61.
Lippi, Filippino, Madonna crowned by angels, 45, Adoration of the Magi, 45-46, Death of Lucretia, 140, Holy Family, 140, fresco, St. Paul and St. Peter in prison, Martyrdom of St. Peter, 222, 223, Madonna, 232, Madonna appearing to St. Bernard, 233.
Lippi, Filippo, Madonna and Child, 36-37, Madonna and Child, 138-139, Annunciation, 218.
Lippo Memmi (see Memmi, Lippo).
Loggia of the Bigallo, 4, 5.
Loggia dei Lanzi, 1, 3, 5-9.
Loggia de' Priori, 4.
Loggia della Signoria, 4.
Lorenzetti, Pietro, Madonna, 16, Anchorites in the Desert, 16-17.
Lorenzo, Bicci di (see Bicci di Lorenzo).
Lorenzo di Credi, Christ and the Magdalen, 34, Christ and the Woman of Samaria, 35, Annunciation, 35-36, Madonna and Child, 37, Annunciation, 38, Madonna and St. John, 38-39, Venus, 51, portraits, 52, 62, Virgin adoring the Child, 88.
Lorenzo Lotto (see Lotto, Lorenzo).
Lorenzo Monaco, Pietà, 22, Adoration of the Magi, 23, Tabernacle, 23-24, altarpiece, Coronation of the Virgin, 85-87, Madonna and Child, 185-188, frescoes, history of the Virgin, 230.
Lotto, Lorenzo, Holy Family, 78-79, Three Ages of Man, 124.
Lucas van Leyden (see Leyden, Lucas van).
Luca Signorelli, 28-29, Holy Family, 39, Holy Family, 140-141.
Luini, the Daughter of Herodias, 63.

Mainardi, figures of saints, 32.
Majano, Benedetto da (see Benedetto da Majano).
Mantegna, portrait of the Duchess of Urbino, 59, 63, triptych, 73-74, 76.
Mariotto Albertinelli (see Albertinelli, Mariotto).

Martini, Simone (see Memmi, Simone Martini).

Marzocco, 5.

Masaccio, portrait, 56, fresco, Adam and Eve driven from Eden, 221, Tribute Money, 222–223, Shadow of Peter, St. Peter Baptising, St. Peter and St. John distributing alms, 224, Consecration of the Church, 225.

Masolino, fresco, Adam and Eve in Paradise, 221, Cure of Petronilla, 222, Preaching of St. Peter, 223, 224.

Matsys, Quintin, portrait, 111.

Medici, rise of the, 3.

Medici, Cosimo de' (see Cosimo I. and Cosimo Pater Patriæ).

Medici, Giovanni de', monument of, 218.

Medici, Giuliano di, Duke of Nemours, monument of, 220.

Medici, Giulio de', Cardinal, portrait of, 132.

Medici, Ippolito de', portrait of, 113.

Medici, Lorenzo de', Duke of Urbino, monument of, 220.

Medici, Piero de', portrait head of, 172, bust of, 176, monument of, 218.

Memling, portraits, 65, Enthroned Madonna, 66–67.

Memmi, Lippo, altar-piece, Annunciation, 18–19.

Memmi, Simone Martini, altar-piece, Annunciation, 18–19.

Metzu, 64.

Michael Angelo Buonarotti, figure of David by, 5, Holy Family, 61–62, Dying Adonis, 148, Victory, 148, bust of Brutus, 150, Madonna and Child, 150, Masque of a Satyr, 151, Bacchus, 151, Leda, reduction of, 151, bust of, 165, David, 176, copies of the David and figures from the Medici tombs, 193, fortress, 194, Medici tombs, 215, 220, 236.

Michelozzo, court of the Palazzo Vecchio, 5, St. John the Baptist, 162, John the Baptist, 171, St. Matthew, 181–182, design of chapel, 196, design of baldacchino, 228.

Mieris, 64.

Milano, Giovanni da (see Giovanni da Milano).

Millais, portrait of himself, 92.

Mino da Fiesole, Virgin and Child, 175, Cupid, 175, Tabernacle, 175, Madonna and Child, 176, tombs, 233.

Monaco, Don Lorenzo (see Lorenzo Monaco).

Montelupo, Baccio da (see Baccio da Montelupo).

Mor, Anthony, portrait, 66.

Moretto, portrait of a Man with a Guitar, 81.

Moroni, portrait, 74, portrait, 82, 122, 124.

Murillo, Madonna and Child, 130.

Index.

Nanni di Banco (see Banco, Nanni di).
National Museum (see Bargello).
Neri di Bicci, Annunciation, 25, Madonna, 26, 35, Annunciation, 229.
Niccolò d'Arezzo, sculptured Annunciation, 182.
Niccolò di Piero Gerini, Coronation of the Madonna, 20.
Niccolò di Piero Lamberti, 147.
Nicolas Froment (see Froment, Nicolas).

Ognissanti, church of, 233.
Opera, Giovanni dell' (see Giovanni dell' Opera).
Orcagna, design of the Loggia dei Lanzi, 3, design of the Loggia of the Bigallo, 4, figure of Music, 171, shrine, 178, same, 184–185, 236.
Or San Michele, 3, 176–189.

Palazzo del Podestà (see Bargello).
Palazzo degli Uffizi (see Uffizi Palace).
Palazzo Vecchio, 1–5.
Palma Vecchio, Holy Family, 81, Judith, 82, 127, Holy Family, 135.
Paolo di Stefano, frescoes, 196.
Paolo Uccello (see Uccello, Paolo).
Paolo Veronese (see Veronese, Paolo).
Parigi, Alfonso, completion of the Uffizi, 9.

Paris Bordone (see Bordone, Paris).
Parmigianino, Madonna and Child, 110.
Paul III., portrait of, 137–138.
Perugino, Madonna and Child, 60, 62, 92, Madonna adoring the Child, 112, Entombment, 119, Magdalen, 131, Madonna and Child, 138, Assumption of the Madonna, 228, Madonna and Saints, 229, Crucifixion, 236–237.
Pesellino, Annunciation, 26.
Petrus Cristus, portraits, 69.
Piazza della Signoria, 1–11.
Piazzale Michelangiolo, 193.
Piero della Francesca, portraits, 34–35, portrait of Beatrice d'Este, 138.
Piero di Cosimo, Marriage of Perseus, 28, Andromeda, 29, Madonna, 29, 55.
Piero di Giovanni Tedesco, 147, 183.
Piero Gerini, Niccolò di (see Niccolò di Piero Gerini).
Pietro da Cortona, frescoes, 136.
Pietro Lorenzetti (see Lorenzetti, Pietro).
Pietro Tacca (see Tacca, Pietro).
Pinturicchio, Adoration of the Magi, 138.
Piombo, Sebastiano del (see Sebastiano del Piombo).
Pisano, Andrea, 184.
Pisano, Niccolò, interior of Santa Trinità, 229, 238–239.

Index.

Pistoia, Gerino da (see Gerino da Pistoia).
Pitti Palace, 107–144.
  Apollo, Sala d', 129–132.
  Educazione di Giove, Stanza dell', 134–136.
  Flora, Stanza di, 143.
  Giove, Sala di, 122–125.
  Giustizia, Stanza della, 143.
  Iliade, Sala dell', 109–115.
  Marte, Sala di, 125–128.
  Poccetti, Stanza del, 142.
  Prometeo, Stanza di, 138–142.
  Putti, Stanza dei, 143–144.
  Saturno, Sala di, 115–121.
  Stufa, Stanza della, 136.
  Ulisse, Stanza di, 136–138.
Podestà, 145–146.
Polidoro Veneziano (see Veneziano, Polidoro).
Pollaiolo, Antonio, figures of Virtues, 28, St. James, St. Vincent, and St. Eustace, 33–34, Prudence, 40–41, Ecce Homo, 141, St. Sebastian, 142, Annunciation, 200, frescoes, 200.
Ponte Vecchio, 108.
Pontormo, portrait of Cosimo I., 42–43, portrait of Cosimo Pater Patriæ, 43, 45, St. Anthony, 110, Santi Coronati, 115, Adoration of the Magi, 142, Visitation, 227.
Pordenone, portrait of, 70, 131.
Porta San Giorgio, 238.
Portinari, Folco, founder of the Hospital of Santa Maria Nuova, 235.
Praxiteles, 101.

Puvis de Chavannes, portrait, 92.

Quintin Matsys (see Matsys, Quintin).

Raffaello di Franco, Entombment, 46–47.
Raphael, 9, Madonna del Cardellino, 57, St. John in the Desert, 57–58, the Fornarina, 58–59, portrait of Julius II., 59, 92, La Gravida, 110, Madonna del Granduca, 116, portraits of Angiolo and Maddalena Doni, 116–117, Vision of Ezekiel, 117, portrait of Cardinal Inghirami, 117–118, Madonna del Baldacchino, 118, portrait of Cardinal Bibbiena, 120, Madonna della Sedia, 120–121, Holy Family, 126, portrait of Julius II., 128, Madonna della Lucertola (copy), 130, portrait of Pope Leo X., 131–132, 133, La Velata, 135, Last Supper, 234.
Rembrandt, portrait of himself, 130, Old Man, 133.
Reni, Guido (see Guido Reni).
Ridolfo Ghirlandajo (see Ghirlandajo, Ridolfo).
Robbia, della, various works, 166–169, 171, Crucifixion, Liberation of St. Peter, 175, 183, 200.
Robbia, Andrea della, reliefs, 237.
Robbia, Giovanni della, Pietà, 194.

Robbia, Luca della, Madonna and Child, 180.
Romano, Giulio, Apollo and the Muses, 119, copy of Raphael's Madonna della Lucertola, 130, 132.
Rosa, Salvator, 133, portrait, 136, 144.
Rosselli, Cosimo, Coronation of the Virgin, 27, Adoration of the Magi, 27, Madonna and Child, 47, fresco, San Filippo Benizzi, 277.
Rosselli, Matteo, Triumph of David, 133.
Rossellino, Antonio, tabernacle for the elements, 151, St. John, 172, bust, 172, bust of Francesco Sassetti, 173, Virgin and Child, 174, St. John, 174, Madonna adoring the Child, 174–175, Chapel of St. James, 199–200.
Rossi, Ludovico de', Cardinal, portrait of, 132.
Rossi, Rosso, 115, Three Fates, 124, fresco of Justice, 167, Marriage of the Virgin, 219.
Rosso Fiorentino (see Fiorentino, Rosso).
Rovezzano, Benedetto da (see Benedetto da Rovezzano).
Rubens, 59, portrait of his wife, 60, 92, Holy Family, 110, Holy Family, 122, 125, Effects of War, 126, portrait of himself and his brother and Lipsius and Grotius, 126–127, landscape, 133, portrait of the Duke of Buckingham, 137.
Rustici, Death of the Magdalen, 134.

Salvator Rosa (see Rosa, Salvator).
Sangallo, Giuliano da (see Giuliano da Sangallo).
San Leonardo, church of, 237–240.
San Lorenzo, church of, 215–220, Old Sacristy, 217–218, New Sacristy, 219–220, Cappella dei Principi, 219–220.
San Miniato, 190–203.
Sansovino, portrait of, 80.
Sansovino, Christ in Glory, 165, Bacchus, 176.
Santa Maria Nuova, Hospital of, 235–236.
Santa Trinità, church of, 229–232.
Santo Spirito, church of, 232–233.
Sarto, Andrea del (see Andrea del Sarto).
Savoldo, Transfiguration, 83.
Savonarola, 4.
Scarselino, Birth of a Noble Infant, 143.
Schauffelein, Crucifixion of St. Peter, 67.
Sebastiano del Piombo, Fornarina, 58–59, Death of Adonis, 78, portrait, 79, Martyrdom of St. Agatha, 115–116.
Settignano, Desiderio da (see Desiderio da Settignano).

Siena, Guido da (see Guido da Siena).
Siena, Ugolino da (see Ugolino da Siena).
Signorelli, Luca (see Luca Signorelli).
Signoria, 2-3.
Simone di Francesco Talenti, completion of the Loggia dei Lanzi, 3.
Simone, Francesco di (see Francesco di Simone).
Simone Martini Memmi (see Memmi, Simone Martini).
Sodoma, Martyrdom of St. Sebastian, 48, 54, 60.
Spagnoletto, Flaying of St. Bartholomew, 132.
Spinello Aretino, 23, 87, frescoes, 196, altar-piece, 196-197, frescoes, 201-203, frescoes, life of St. Cecilia, 224-225.
Stefano, Paolo di (see Paolo di Stefano).
Strozzi, Zanobi, portrait of Giovanni de' Medici, 24, St. Lawrence, 24.
Sustermans, Holy Family, 110, portrait of a Prince of Denmark, 114, portrait of a Medici infant, 139.

Tacca, Pietro, 94.
Taddeo Gaddi (see Gaddi, Taddeo).
Talenti, Simone, sculptured figures, 149.
Teniers, 67.
Tinelli, Tiberio, portrait, 135.

Tintoretto, Domenico, portrait, 71, St. Augustine, 72, Leda, 72, portrait, 80, portrait of Sansovino, 80, Marriage at Cana, 83, Sacrifice of Isaac, 83, portrait, 122, portrait of Luigi Cornaro, 127, 130, Venus and Vulcan, 133, Madonna and Child, 137.
Titian, 10, Venus, 59, Venus, 61, portrait of Beccadelli, 61, portraits of the Duke and Duchess of Urbino, 71, Flora, 71-72, portrait of Caterina Cornaro, 74, Madonna and Child, 80, Battle of Cadore, copy of, 80, Madonna and Child, 80-81, Madonna, 81, Madonna and Child, 82-83, 92, Christ, 110, portrait, 112, portrait of Cardinal Ippolito de' Medici, 113, portrait of Philip II., 113, portrait group, 115, Bacchanal, copy, 120, La Bella, 122, Young Man with the Glove, 125, portrait of Luigi Cornaro, 127, portrait of Vesalius, 127, Magdalen, 129, portrait of Pietro Aretino, 131, Madonna and Child, 133, portrait of a Duke of Ferrara, 137, portrait of Pope Paul III., 137-138.
Tito, Tiberio, 131.
Torbido, portrait of Gattamelata, 72-73.
Tribolo, Niccolò, copies of Michael Angelo's Night, Dawn, etc.

Index.

Uccello, Paolo, battle painting, 25.
Uffizi Palace, 8–106.
  Dutch School, Hall of the, 64.
  Flemish and German Schools, Halls of the, 64–69.
  French School, Hall of the, 69.
  Italian Masters, Hall of the, 63.
  Long Corridor, 12–30.
  Portico, 9.
  Sculpture, 93–106.
  Tribuna, 56–63.
  Tuscan Halls, 31–56.
  Venetian School, Halls of the, 70–83.
Ugolino da Siena, Madonna, 178, same, 185–186.

Vacca, Flaminio, figure of a lion, 8.
Van Cleef, Joost, Mater Dolorosa, 67.
Van der Goes, Madonna and Child, 67, Madonna, 156, triptych, 235–236.
Van der Helst, 92, portrait, 135.
Van der Werf, 64.
Van der Weyden, Roger, Deposition, 65.
Van Dyck, 59, 62, 92, portrait of Charles I. and Henrietta Maria, 120, portrait of Cardinal Bentivoglio, 128, portrait of the Duke of Buckingham, 137.
Van Eyck, Jan, Adoration of the Magi, 68–69.

Vasari, façade of the Palazzo Vecchio, 2, erection of the Uffizi, 8–9, portrait of Lorenzo the Magnificent, 42, St. Jerome, 143.
Vecchietta, Lorenzo, statue for a tomb, 164.
Vecchio, Palma (see Palma Vecchio).
Velasquez, 92, portrait, 113, portrait of Philip IV., 135.
Veneziano, Domenico, Madonna and Child, 87.
Veneziano, Polidoro, Madonna and Child, 79.
Veronese, Carletto, Madonna, 70.
Veronese, Paolo, Holy Family, 59, Esther before Ahasuerus, 71, 77–78, St. Catherine, 79, Crucifixion, 80, Martyrdom of St. Justina, 82, portrait, 112, St. Benedict, 113, Baptism of Christ, 114, 122.
Vesalius, portrait of, 127.
Verrocchio, fountain by, 5, David, 162–163, head of Piero de' Medici, 172, relief from the tomb of Francesca Pitti Tornabuoni, 173–174, Virgin and Child, 174, portrait statue, 174, Christ and Thomas, 179, fountain, 218, monument of Piero de' Medici, 218.
Vetulonia, objects from, 205–206.
Vinci, Leonardo da (see Leonardo da Vinci).

Vinci, Pierino da, reliefs, 150–151.

Volterra, Daniele da (see Daniele da Volterra).

Watts, portrait of himself, 92.

Zanobi Strozzi (see Strozzi, Zanobi).

Zelotti, Annunciation, 77–78.

Zucchero, Magdalen, 139.